DAVID NICKSON & SUZY SIDDONS
NO FIGHTING IN THE KITCHEN

For our dear Kevin.
Who has *never* fought in our kitchen.

All our love!

David + Suzy

xxx

And Fatima + Bonzo

DAVID NICKSON & SUZY SIDDONS

NO FIGHTING IN THE KITCHEN

NEW ENGLISH LIBRARY

British Library Cataloguing in Publication Data

Nickson, David
No fighting in the kitchen.
1. Cookery
I. Title II. Siddons, Suzy
241.5

ISBN 0-450-54401-X

Copyright © David Nickson and Suzy Siddons 1990
Illustrations by Roger Wade-Walker

First published in Great Britain 1990

All rights reserved. No part of this publication may be reproduced or transmitted in any form or by any means, electronic or mechanical, including photocopying, recording, or any information storage and retrieval system, without either prior permission in writing from the publisher or a licence, permitting restricted copying. In the United Kingdom such licences are issued by the Copyright Licensing Agency, 33–34 Alfred Place, London WC1E 7DP. The right of David Nickson and Suzy Siddons to be identified as the author of this work has been asserted by them in accordance with the Copyright, Designs and Patents Act 1988.

Published by New English Library,
a division of Hodder and Stoughton Ltd,
Mill Road, Dunton Green, Sevenoaks, Kent TN13 2YA
Editorial Office: 47 Bedford Square, London WC1B 3DP.

Photoset in Linotron Baskerville by
Rowland Phototypesetting Ltd, Bury St Edmunds, Suffolk

Printed in Great Britain by
St Edmundsbury Press Ltd, Bury St Edmunds, Suffolk

To Mrs C. V. Nickson

Contents

		Foreword	ix
Chapter	1	Kitchen Layout and Equipment	1
	2	Planning and Shopping	11
	3	Wine? Why Not!	25
	4	Two People, One Kitchen	43
	5	Serving It Up	51
	6	Guz-Before	61
	7	Guz-in-the-Middle	71
	8	Guz-After	85
	9	Dinner Party Games	95
	10	Sunday Lunch	103
	11	Stodgy Puddings	115
	12	Disasters and How to Recover from Them	123
	13	Know Your Guests	131
		Acknowledgements	137
Appendix A		Weights and Measures	139
Appendix B		Safety First in the Kitchen	143
		Index	149

Foreword

How the book came about

There seems to be less and less time to do more and more. What's worse, people expect to be entertained with food that would not disgrace the best of restaurants. We entertain a lot, and by practice, trial and (often) error have discovered how to produce good food easily.

We didn't realise how expert we had become until someone said they were really looking forward to having us round for dinner, but 'would we mind if it wasn't till next month, as they didn't think they could get time off work to prepare'. Although we said nothing at the time, after they left and we were having the usual dinner-party post mortem, we thought it was very odd to need time off to do a meal. The seed of an idea was planted. The seed got watered two nights later when we went to a couple of our acquaintance (that meant that she was a friend but we hadn't met her new boyfriend) for supper. We arrived ten minutes late (as is deemed polite) to find that there was mayhem in the kitchen. It seemed that our friend's partner (as they are called these days) had commented adversely on the quality of the lettuce that she had procured on her way home from the office. This had been the last straw apparently and the lady in question retorted forcibly. He then threw the offending vegetable at the wall where it made a dull impact prior to gravity taking its course. Not to be outdone, and being a spirited girl, she settled the dispute by rubbing the remains into his face. It was at about this point that we had arrived, or a food fight of momentous proportions might have ensued. We noticed there was a bit of an atmosphere when we were let in (like cats that have had a disagreement you couldn't get both of them in the same room for any extended period of time) and this state of affairs continued until supper was actually served. It was not until after the coffee and brandy stage that the full story emerged. The meal had been edible but that is all. However, out of this meal our seed began to grow and *No Fighting in the Kitchen* was born.

We realised that what we took for granted was actually rarer than we thought. As we both make part of our livings from scribbling, we knew that a book had thrust itself upon us. We didn't want to write yet another cookbook with the same old recipe ideas reworked to fit a new marketing niche. We wanted to write something which would encompass the complete subject of mealtime entertaining. We wanted to give people skills, not formulae. What's more we wanted to make people laugh. Well, we hope that we have succeeded and that you will enjoy *No Fighting in the Kitchen*. So seconds away, Round 1.

Chapter 1

Kitchen Layout and Equipment
or
A Bad WorkMAN Always Blames HER Tools

> **If the combatants are to stand a fighting chance in the kitchen war, then the battlefield must be carefully planned and each participant needs to be properly armed.**

The Theatre of War – the Kitchen

The most successful generals always select the site of the battlefield to suit themselves and their armies. The same applies to a working kitchen. This doesn't mean that you need to spend phenomenal sums of money on a new kitchen (unless you think it will make you feel better, or you want to impress the neighbours), but that basic kitchen organisation is an essential for a peaceful working area if two people are going to cook in it.

THE CORNERSTONES OF THE KITCHEN

These are the sink, the rubbish bin, the cooker and the refrigerator.

In any kitchen there will be 'givens' (usually expensive) such as where the plumbing is, where the windows and doors are and that funny box halfway up the wall which is something to do with the heating. As a rule, these are impractical to change and you just have to plan round them. An example of how a kitchen can be improved is Suzy's first kitchen. The diagram shows how it was laid out originally. It was a nightmare to work in – it was so small that when you shut the door you got claustrophobia. When you opened the door you couldn't get at the oven. The oven caused the refrigerator all sorts of grief and most of the cupboard and working space was useless. It was substantially improved by replacing the door with a bead blind, swapping the cooker with the refrigerator, putting up a wire grid rack to hang implements on and providing hanging hooks for the pots and pans. This cost very little – a good thing as Suzy was a student at the time.

(Something I didn't know was that most refrigerators have reversible doors – this could have saved me a great deal of anguish. – S.)

A few words about minimum space. Two people can cook in a remarkably small space, but you need at least ten feet by eight feet of floor space for comfort. Obviously more space than this makes life easier, unless the kitchen is so large that you need telephones to talk to each other and roller skates for commuting.

(Which enthusiastic washer-uppers? – S.)

(If you have a wide enough windowsill you can grow herbs in pots on it, and the fact that you see them each time you use the taps means that you will remember to water them regularly – S.)

There are common-sense factors to consider. Don't have the refrigerator next to the cooker, not unless you want the fridge defrosted as the Sunday lunch cooks; nor do you want the sink next to the cooker, as boiling pans are prone to being upset by enthusiastic washer-uppers.

However once you have dealt with these immovables it all comes down to working areas.

The sink should be placed under a window (it usually is). This gives you something to look at/jump out of/throw things through when it is your turn to do the washing-up.

The type of sink is important too – a double sink will make life easier, and one of those squirty things like a shower attachment makes rinsing things a matter of seconds. Lever action taps similar to those found in hospitals are simpler to operate and a must for old, disabled or just plain rheumaticky folk. Make sure you have somewhere handy to keep dishcloths/mops by the sink, and remember to keep a roll of kitchen towel nearby for general tidying operations.

You will need a good working space each, preferably on opposite sides of the kitchen (or ends if it is long and narrow). These spaces need to be well lit, have plenty of power points and good access to the sink and the waste-bin. An L-shaped working space is ideal. You stand in the corner and have plenty of space within reach without having to move very far (though very long work surfaces can help keep you fit).

If you can manage it, have the refrigerator and the cooker on opposite sides and at one end of the kitchen. This will make it much easier for you both to get at them. The other important item is the rubbish bin. Large flip-top ones which take big black bin-liners are

3

best. Try not to keep the bin hidden away in a cupboard; it may be nice to have an invisible bin, but the kitchen is a work place and it really is a nuisance to have to keep opening doors every time you want to throw away the potato peelings. This bin should be located in an area of the kitchen where you can both get at it without having to become contortionists.

WORKTOPS, FLOORS AND WALLS

If you have a really large kitchen then a centre work island can be installed. This will make coordinated cooking much easier as you can have the active cooking area well out of everyone's way in the middle of the room and you then have the other four sides of the room for work surfaces/washing-up areas and so on. Kitchens like this are heaven.

The materials you use for the worktops, floor and wall coverings are very important too. They have to be easy to clean or you will spend all your time scrubbing or being sick with food poisoning.

There are other aspects to consider as well. Ceramic floors are very hygienic and look wonderful, but they come to grief if you drop a heavy pan and can be extremely dangerous when wet. Carpet is a disaster, although there are some special rubber-backed, short-woven pile ones that will survive – but things have a habit of getting ground in after a while. Our favourite flooring is cushioned lino either from a roll or in tiles.

Work surfaces should be covered in some sort of heat-resistant material. Walls should be painted with an easy-wipe silk/eggshell finish or tiled. Wallpaper should be avoided in the kitchen; it tends to peel, and even the specialist papers are wont to come adrift and get tatty. The kitchen is a tough working environment which is full of steam, water, detergent, oven cleaner, heat and sharp implements.

STORAGE

Storage is vital. You simply can't have too much of it. Don't forget to have special storage racks for fresh vegetables. A useful way of creating extra storage is to hang things up, either on grids on the wall or from hooks/chains to the ceiling (though this may be a little tricky with tall people bumping their heads or short people being unable to reach).

Given that you've got the space, what sort of storage do you need for what? The table below covers most requirements:

Item	Storage requirements
Meat, Offal, Poultry, Fish, Cheese, Milk, Eggs	Refrigerator – it is better to keep meat, fish, etc. in separate airtight containers. Avoid plastic bags as the condensation is bad news.
Vegetables	Salad compartment of refrigerator, or the coolest part of the kitchen. Better still a larder. Vegetables should not be all squashed together. Remove from plastic bags to prevent them from turning to soup with condensation, and keep them out of direct sunlight (especially chicory and root vegetables).
Fresh fruit	Preferably buy it and eat it; don't store it. The refrigerator is the best place. Place fruit so that it is not squashed up. An airtight container is a good idea as well, then it should keep for a couple of days or so. Citrus fruits keep well in a bowl – their thick skins protect them.
Herbs	Crumbled, dried herbs can be kept in jars in a space rack. Fresh herbs (unless they are growing in pots) don't keep very well. Herbs can be frozen either in ice cubes or loose and then dried on kitchen paper in a shady place. Best of all, you can grow your own easily in a window box, on a balcony, or in a small patch in the garden.

Larder goods By which we mean tinned stuff, jam, dried fruit, salt, pepper, curry powder, vinegars, cooking wine, and so forth. Dark but airy cupboards are ideal. A good idea is to use lots of plastic baskets to organise the space, e.g. one for spices, one for jams, one for baking and so on. This makes it easy to find things and to keep clean.

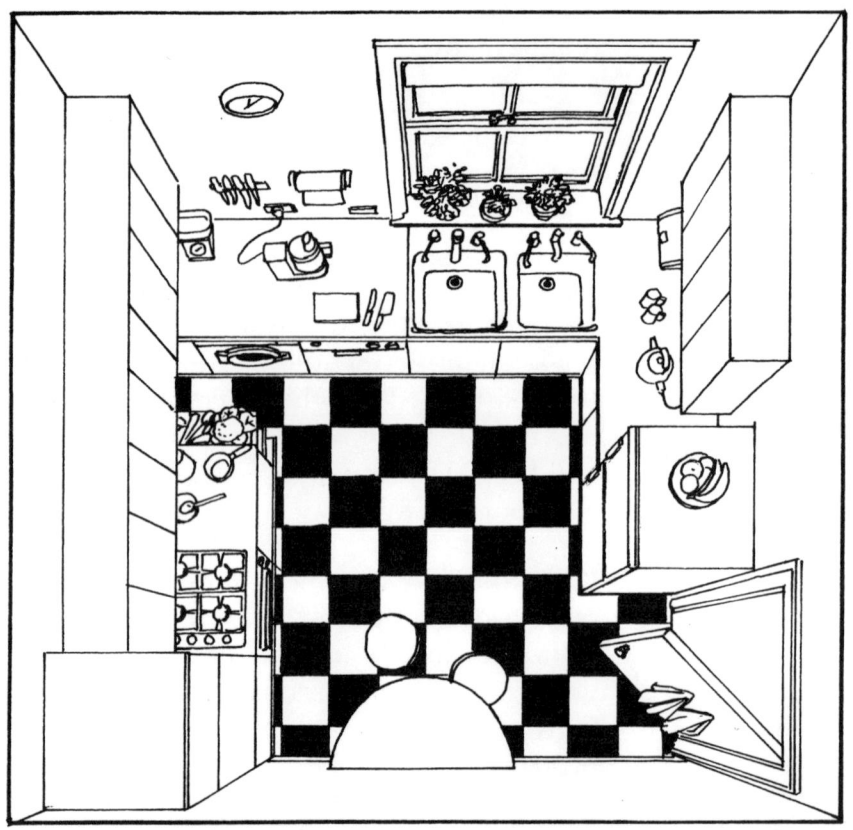

The diagram shows how our kitchen is laid out. It is by no means the last word in spiffy kitchens, but it provides all the essentials for two people to prepare and cook food together. What's more, it *does* work.

We have two main work spaces on either side of the kitchen. Both are well supplied with electric power and light. One is convenient for the cooker and the other for the refrigerator. The rubbish bin is under the semicircular table and is easy to get at. The sink (double) is under the window and has additional working space to one side of it (useful for putting things out of the way). We find that this kitchen works well for two people. However, on odd occasions when a guest has arrived early and insisted on helping, we have discovered that three's a crowd and there's always someone where you want to be, using something you want to use.

Equipment

Kitchen equipment comes in four categories, essential, desirable, frivolous and pointless. Every kitchen should have something from each category. You can then use the pointless items for throwing at each other without impairing your cooking potential. As a rule, it is much better to have the minimum set of equipment of high quality and add to it later, than to have a lot of low quality items straight away.

Let's start with essentials. You need an oven and a hob with four rings, a refrigerator and a sink!

Three saucepans, an 8 pint (5 litre) casserole (preferably oval if it's the only one), old-fashioned scales, measuring jugs, ladle, slotted spoon, wooden spoons (2), tin opener, rolling pin, kitchen clock, balloon whisk, frying pan with lid (of solid construction, useful for bringing partner to heel), roasting tins (large and small), wire mesh strainer, carving knife with steel and fork (with guard), serrated-edged kitchen knife, kettle (preferably electric jug type), a square-shaped grater, mixing bowls (large and medium), corkscrew (vital – make sure you have a spare), wooden chopping board, pepper mill.

(I firmly maintain that each cook should have their favourite knife which should never be used or sharpened by anyone else, and if I ever catch David using mine, this is grounds for severe reparations. – S.)

Now for desirables. The dishwasher has to come top of the list of these. We lived for the first two years of our married life without one – it was a continual bone of contention. Suzy likes to leave washing-up for a while,

(Especially since it washes the back of the plates and the bottoms of the wine glasses properly, something that David appears to find unnecessary. – S.)

one or two weeks at least, I like to do it ASAP. This meant that a disproportionate amount of washing-up was done by me – a serious strain on the relationship. We haven't looked back since.

Another desirable is a steamer/saucepan combination. These wonderful widgets comprise a stainless steel pan with a number of steamer pans (with holes in them to allow steam to pass through) which stack up on top of each other, and a lid. These are so good we think they could almost be considered essential. You can boil potatoes in the base and steam carrots, peas, cabbage and so on in the steamer pans. You can add the steamer layers at different times to suit the food being cooked – what's more it only uses up one ring.

A good quality food processor is also a major boon when preparing food; it will save you a lot of time and effort. Those hand-held blenders, of the same type as the Braun Multipractic, are extremely useful too. We use ours more than the food processor, especially for soups and pâté. A separate grill and toaster are good news as well.

You can also get a squirty thing, a sort of shower attachment for the sink, which is perfect for rinsing things down. These are very useful for those with a dishwasher.

Frivolous items are the things that make the kitchen yours. They can be useful too but not essential. Shape-cutters can be useful for both pastry and bread. Why have boring shaped toast when you can have stars, hearts and flowers? Or perhaps one of those vacuum action widgets for preserving half-consumed bottles of wine . . .

(Not a frequent problem. – S.)

(David firmly believes an egg separator to be an essential item, but surely that's what eggshells are for? – S.)

Pointless items. These are to be found in every kitchen. We have a peculiar little circular thing at the bottom of the sink which serves no purpose as far as anyone can tell but it's been there since we moved in. We have also heard of electric carving knives . . .

Golden Rules for the kitchen of our dreams

Rule 1   Have the sink by the window

Rule 2   Keep the cooker and the refrigerator well apart

Rule 3   Try to have two separate working spaces

Rule 4   You can't have too many power points

Rule 5   Cupboards

Rule 6   More cupboards

Rule 7   Have the right equipment

Rule 7a Have good quality equipment

Rule 8   Make sure there is plenty of light

Rule 9   Make it easy to keep clean

Chapter 2

Planning and Shopping
or
I Didn't Invite Them in the First Place

> **Campaign Planning, Armaments and Rations.**
>
> **This is the key to success. Whether you have thirty minutes or thirty days before your guests are due to arrive, it is planning that will get you through without tears before bedtime.**

Tools

Diary, record of meals, phone numbers of guests, pen and paper for shopping lists, excuses list, recipe books, drink. The strength of the drink depends on the nature of the event. (If your partner has just come home and mentioned that six people are arriving for supper in an hour's time, then a double Scotch is justified – and a meat cleaver.) Things to nibble aren't a bad idea either – reading recipe books is hungry work.

Guests

(Why is it that when you invite vegetarians you are expected to provide a vegetarian meal, and yet when carnivores are invited by vegetarians, meat is hardly ever served? – S.)

First choose your guests and establish any limiting factors. Are they vegetarian?

Do they have any allergies? What are they? Do they have to leave by a particular time? Will you *want* them to leave by any particular time? Do they have children? What will the children eat? If they have children, make sure you know what needs to be done with them – boiling in oil or spiking the baby's bottle with gin can often offend. Now is when you look in your little book to find out what you fed them last time – repeating the same meal is almost as boring as repeating the same old anecdotes. If you are sending formal invitations, now is a good time to decide who is responsible for writing and posting them.

Battle Planning

With the guest list drawn up, now the battle planning and shopping plan can start. The purpose of this is to make sure that you know what it is you need to do and when you need to do it and who is going to do it. A few minutes spent early on will save hours of strife on the night. The idea is that if you must fight, then fight over the planning, not over the cooker.

Now establish *your* limiting factors: How long have you got? Are the shops open? What have we got in the fridge? And so on . . . This will save you from embarrassing moments such as offering garlic to a vampire or, worse, having to produce a five-course dinner in twenty minutes. The latter situation has been cited under mental cruelty in a divorce petition in the USA.

The next stage is to choose what you are going to cook. This is the creative part – you know what you can't do; now choose from what you can do. Tailor the meal to the time available, the occasion and the company expected. Now work out what ingredients you are going to need and make a list of what you don't already have. This often leads to some interesting discoveries, particularly in the backs of cupboards. We still have some tinned oysters (yuck) which we have kept 'just in case' for at least five years, and neither of us can eat shellfish.

(And what about the bottle of 'excellent Bordeaux, but corked' that you have been intending to use as wine vinegar for three years then? – S.)

Another thing to bear in mind is the colour balance of the meal. Once upon a time in Weybridge we were served an all white meal: mushroom soup, fish with mashed potato and parsley sauce, cauliflower and a choice of ice cream or rice pudding. The hotel had once been a nursing home, it seems, and this had left its mark on the catering.

GATHERING

Gathering comes next. In prehistoric times (before we had Radio 4), mankind eked out his existence as a hunter-gatherer; it was a battle of wits between man and beast. Having been to Marks and Sparks on a Friday evening, we don't think that things have changed all that much except that the shopping trolley has replaced the beast. You already have a list of what is needed, so all you have to do now is decide who gathers what and when. It is a good idea to organise the shopping list by the shops that you will use, e.g. grocer, butcher, greengrocer, chemist, hardware, psychiatrist (in case you have any problems you need fixed before the guests arrive).

SHOPPING

We usually decide who does the shopping on the basis that whoever has the best reason for not doing it, does it. They can then reward themselves with a sulk or a grump.

(I don't agree with David here – supermarkets are amazing nowadays with a superb selection of excellently chosen merchandise and the advantage of only needing one vast trek per week aided by wheeled vehicles – both cars and trollies. They are also open in the evening and there is no need to rush from shop to shop in order to restock on all the things your partner has eaten from the storecupboard during your absence and forgotten to replace. – S.)

Shopping is an art form and the key to success is the shops themselves. The ideal is to have a comprehensive row of local shops; a butcher, a greengrocer, a baker (usually a patisserie today), and a general store. A fishmonger is a rare bonus. The supermarkets are a poor alternative to having your own shops who will order meat specially for you and butcher it to suit, tell you which vegetables are a good buy and generally make life easier for you. We're very lucky in having just such a row of shops within a couple of minutes' walk in our part of London. It is impossible to overestimate the value of a good butcher and his knowledge when you're buying meat. He is worth his weight in gold.

13

To help you, here are some suggestions about what to look out for when buying meat, fish, cheese, and vegetables. A good way to shop when you don't have to be totally committed to a specific menu, is to choose what looks best in the butcher's, greengrocer's, and so forth, and then think up a menu to use up what you've bought. It may not be the best balanced meal possible, but the quality of the ingredients is more than half the battle when cooking. What's more you'll get a good meal.

Meat

Meat is by far the most difficult food to buy. We asked our butcher to give us the benefit of his experience for this book, as we always rely on him to get us what we want, and he's always right. This is what he advises: free-range and 'organic' produce does have better flavour and is generally of a higher quality than factory-farmed meat. It costs a little more and can sometimes be hard to find, but it is well worth it.

Beef

The carcass is usually hung by the butcher for a fortnight before it is jointed and sold. This is important as the meat would be very tough and lacking in flavour if this was not done. Beef should be a deep rich red and the fat should be cream coloured. Lean cuts should be lightly marbled with fat if they are not to be too dry when cooked. Joints of beef will keep for up to four days when refrigerated. (Minced beef should be cooked on the day it is purchased.) You should avoid bright red meat which may not have been hung properly and will not have a good flavour. Similarly avoid very dark meat with bright yellowish fat as this is probably meat from a dairy herd. This is fine for milk production but is unsuitable for the table.

We are still buying beef on a regular basis despite the BSE (Mad Cow Disease) scares. However, we are careful only to buy organic meat.

Pork

(I am fanatical about how pork or beef are prepared for roasting. More than almost any other meat, pork and beef need attention at the 'butchery' stage. All good butchers will chine or bone a joint for you. This means that the bones are loosely separated from the meat and remain within the joint for roasting [chining] or completely removed [boning] where the meat is roasted without the bones.

I prefer meat that is roasted 'on the bone' since I think this makes the meat tastier. With chining, it is relatively easy to remove the bone before carving. This needs but a little attention before serving. Boned meat usually needs tidying up into a neat shape which, after cooking, is extremely easy to carve [like a loaf of bread]. But some boned meat can be dry, so a moist stuffing needs to be added inside the boned joint.

Scoring is what you do to win points with your pork crackling. Get your butcher to score the rind of the joint at the widths of the slices you will be carving. Narrow intervals are best.)

You don't have to worry about the 'not buying pork during the summer months' advice from your mother any more – refrigeration has seen to that. However, you must always cook pork thoroughly. Never serve it rarer than well done. Good pork is smooth and lean and pale pink, the fat firm and white. If the rind on the fat is left in place for cooking, the rind should be scored. Look at the area where the bone is attached to the meat or exposed to the air; this is the first point that will show deterioration. Avoid pork which is sticky to the touch or carrying too much fat. Pork will keep for up to two days in a refrigerator.

Lamb

This is now hung for as long as beef, about four to five days. Young lamb will be slightly pink and will have a light, white fat cover. It is at its best in the spring. As lambs get older, the meat becomes a darker red and the fat grey coloured. Avoid meat that is like this, or oversized. Lamb joints will keep for up to four days when refrigerated; chops for two days.

Offal

This includes commonplace items such as liver and kidneys, and the more exotic chicken gizzards (used, in Bordeaux, to make the most disgusting regional speciality we have ever encountered) as well as pigs' trotters, calves' feet, tripe, hearts and sweetbreads. Because there is a considerable amount of offal chasing a small number of regular customers (the mind boggles, doesn't it?) you do get some real bargains here. It should be bought fresh, from a reliable source, and since it does not keep, you must cook it the day you buy it.

Poultry

Free-range is first choice, and frozen birds are best avoided. However, the chill-fresh birds from the supermarkets are a good second choice. A good bird will be fresh looking and should have full breasts. A good indication of how tender a bird will be is to press the cartilage at the end of the breast bone. The more supple the better the bird. Avoid birds with yellowish meat (unless they are corn-fed) as this is a sign of old stock.

Fish

This has been making something of a comeback over recent years, whether for health reasons or just because it is good to eat, we don't know. The best fish tends to come from a fishmonger, though the supermarkets are catching up fast. The way to choose a fishmonger is easy. Look at the fish in the window, and see how busy the shop is. Good fresh fish is instantly recognisable, the eyes will be clear, the flesh will be plump and resilient (give it a gentle prod, you should leave no dent), and the gills will be red. If the fish has an excessively fishy smell and doesn't match this description, then it is stale. Don't buy it. It is better to buy fresh frozen fish than stale, not-so-fresh fish. It is very important, both for taste and for health, to get fish home fast, so buy it last on your rounds and into the refrigerator with it as fast as possible. All shellfish should be eaten on the day of purchase as it is the most fickle of fish to buy safely.

(Watch out for warnings in the newspapers about toxins in shellfish. In these days of pollution, some sea beds near industrial outfalls or even coasts where certain algae collect can suddenly become horrifically toxic and shellfish from these areas need to be avoided until the sea becomes clean and the shellfish void these poisons. See our honeymoon story. – S.)

White fish can be kept overnight, smoked fish will keep two or, just maybe, three days. If you don't want everything in the refrigerator to smell of fish, then cover the fish with foil or keep it in one of those resealable plastic bags.

Dairy Produce

This comprises eggs, milk, yoghurt, cream and cheeses. Always look at the 'sell by' date. Again, organic or free-range gives better taste. We usually buy cheeses from a delicatessen or cheese counter that we know and where they let us taste the cheeses before we buy.

Vegetables

With vegetables it is just as important to have them harvested at the right time as it is to have them fresh. Fortunately, most vegetables make it to the shops within a day or two (even overseas produce), so the real question is *when* were they harvested?

Many vegetables need to be harvested young if they are to have the best flavour and texture, so for vegetables like peas, carrots and beans the smaller the better. (Hence the old cannon ball frozen pea advert of old.) Unfortunately, because you pay by the pound, some farmers are tempted to pick late to get a bigger crop. The only way you can influence this is via your greengrocers, by telling them what you want or, less directly, via the supermarket by simply not buying overlarge produce.

You will have to pay more for the smaller produce, at least per pound, but you will find it worthwhile when you come to eat them. You should look for firm young vegetables which have a clear colour to them.

With leaf vegetables such as lettuce, spinach, cabbage, spring greens, cauliflowers, broccoli and leeks, avoid old wilted specimens as they will be crude in flavour or poor in texture. Unlike meat where you can disguise cheap cuts by extra cooking and good sauces, once any vegetable is past its best then that's it; there is nothing you can do about it.

With root vegetables such as parsnips, swedes, celeriac and particularly, potatoes and onions, firmness is the test. Any softness means that they are over the top and likely to get worse when you cook them.

Fruit

Colour, texture, firmness, 'weight in the hand' and smell are the guidelines here. Melons smell really melony when they are ripe, avocados 'give' when you press them at the narrow end, though many have been thoroughly pressed before you get to them and bruising can be confused with ripeness. Ask the greengrocer to choose for you if possible. Pears, peaches and nectarines should smell fruity and give slightly in the hand, apples should feel hard, oranges, lemons and citrus fruit should be firm. Pineapples should give slightly when you wriggle the spiky shoots at the top, grapes should look whole and unwrinkled and feel weighty in the hand. Strawberries, raspberries and any soft fruit sold in containers should be inspected for mould, seepage or bruising before you buy them – hold the container up and look at the base of it – a very revealing exercise! In the main, brown splotches are not a good sign on any fruit as they often show that the produce has been bruised or badly stored.

We wash all vegetables and fruit before we use them but not before we store them as moisture can be a problem during storage.

Meanwhile back at the ranch . . .

Planning the cooking is easy. First decide who cooks what: this can be done on the basis of ability, or, if

(Boring! Boring!! and who has been pushing forward the frontiers of female equality while you've been eating the contents of the storage cupboard? – S.)

you're none too fond of the guests, who knows least about it. Or you can decide on the basis of sensible things such as who has the most time available. (We call that boring, but each to their own.)

You also need to work out the timetable here. When two people are going to use the same kitchen, timings can get tricky, as you almost certainly have only one cooker, for example. In fact, planning how the oven and cooking rings will be used is very important.

(I thought you said that was the easy bit – this was the bit I found the hardest. – S.)

(How true, how true . . . – S.)

Before we got it right we had some fairly serious confrontations and sulks concerning who 'needed' the fourth gas ring when we both wanted it simultaneously. The same thing applies to oven space and oven temperature. You must organise to suit the resources at your disposal and the timescales of the food to be produced. Many things can be prepared in advance and will only need last-minute attention to serve.

Identify the 'time critical' parts of the meal: Here's a list of some of our 'time critical factors': you will no doubt be able to add to these as your stress levels increase:

> Hot soufflés have to be served at exactly the right moment, so the meal must revolve around their needs.
>
> Vegetables are very difficult to keep crisp, but meat can generally rest at least 20 minutes.
>
> Pastry-cased and egg-based tarts which should be 'puffed up' should be served piping hot without waiting.
>
> Yorkshire puddings cannot wait.

Pancakes and crêpes cannot wait.

Once you've taken the ice cream out you're into meltdown.

If you are likely to be pressed for time on the day, review your menu and find alternatives which are not 'time critical'. Choose the right courses and you could turn out a four-course meal with only thirty minutes' work 'on the night'.

Missile delivery

It is a good idea to decide well in advance who is serving what. You really want to be in the situation where one of you is with the guests whilst the other one is performing magic in the kitchen. When you're pushed for time or space on the table, serve up in the kitchen. If you do this, allow extra time for 'display' (arranging food on the plate so that it looks good).

Clearing up is also part of the planning. You need to decide who is going to do the table, clear/load the dishwasher/put into soak/stack up for later, and all the business, like coffee and brandy at the end of the meal whilst everyone else goes to 'sit soft'. The person who does this is traditionally rewarded with a crafty swig at the secret brandy, or whatever else comes to hand.

When you've done all this planning (which might take from thirty seconds for an omelette, to fifteen minutes to half an hour for a dinner party for twelve) you're ready to go. What's more, you stand a very good chance of getting it right, painlessly.

Here's a checklist of questions which you can use to make sure that you've planned for most things.

Limitations: What did we feed them last time?
What did they feed us?

Are they vegetarian?
Do they have allergies (e.g. seafood)?
Any special dietary needs?
Are they (heaven forfend) teetotal?
Are they prone to lateness?
How well do you know them?
Will they be bringing offspring?
If so, how old and how many?
Do they want to leave early?
Do you want them to leave early?

What to cook:
How much time will you have?
What sort of occasion is it?
What is in season?
What suits the weather?
Is it all the same colour (the all white meal)?

Gathering:
What do we have in stock?
What can we buy locally?
Which shops do we need to go to?
What must be bought fresh on the day?
What can you 'make do' with? (e.g. add baking powder to plain flour to get self-raising).

Planning the cooking:
Who will do the shopping?
Who will cook which course?
Who is going to serve the food?
Who will clear up afterwards?
When will the meal be served?
How much oven space do you need? At what temperature?
How many gas/electric rings do you need?
What will take the longest to cook?
What will take the shortest?
What can be kept warm?
What can't be kept warm?
Do things need defrosting?

Serving: Have you got all the cutlery to hand?
Do you have enough serving dishes?
Are the napkins clean/folded/out?
Is there enough space on the table?
Will you have to serve up in the kitchen?
Where are the condiments?
What about 'seconds'?

Clearing up the mess: Who will do it?
What can be done as you go along?
What must be left to soak?
What can be left until later/put in the dishwasher?
Can you teach the cat/dog to do it?
Do you expect to save any leftovers (e.g. for stock, cold meat on Monday, cottage pie, potato cakes, bubble and squeak)?

> "One cannot think well, love well, sleep well, if one has not dined well."
> *Virginia Woolf*

Chapter 3

Wine? Why Not!
or
Toujours les Vins

> **There's a great deal of Botrytis (Noble Rot) talked about wine. But, whatever you think of wine snobs and their 'amusing little wine with just a hint of sarcasm' talk, there is no better complement to a meal than the right wine. After all, wine, women and song are the traditional ingredients for the 'good time' had by the male of the species. For women it is different – wine, men and earplugs! The not-so-common element is that beneficent beverage produced from the fermentation of the fruit of *Vitis vinifera*. In short, wine.**

There are two reasons for buying wine; investment and consumption. For the former you need expert advice, brokers, storage (optional – some investors never even see the stuff; it is just another commodity to their spavin-ridden souls!), deep pockets and a lot of time. For the latter you just need yourself, space, money and the occasional hangover cure.

Wine is made all over the world, it comes in all shapes of containers from tall thin bottles to short, fat, cardboard boxes and at all sorts of prices. It ranges from the sublime (Château Aussone) to the ludicrous (Aunt Matilda's pea-pod Burgundy). It comes in different colours (red to rosé to white), sweetness/dryness, amount of alcohol (from 'Very refreshing this, don't you think?' to 'Come out from under the piano, Henry, the pink elephants left through the French windows ten minutes ago') and still/fizzy.

If all this seems daunting, do not despair! It's really very simple.

Colour

Good wine is never cloudy; it has a pure, clear colour. A first-rate Bordeaux held up to the light will shine like the finest stained glass in the greatest cathedral. Colour is more pronounced in red wines, but some whites have a golden glow reminiscent of honeyed sunshine. With red wines you should tilt the glass and look at the colour where it reaches the rim. If it is purplish then the wine is young and may be a little tough to drink. If it is just right then it will have a distinctly brownish tinge. Rosé wines should have a clear pure colour.

Hint:
A simple, plain wine glass is the best for tasting (and, we think, serving). Avoid the heavily cut crystal stuff. A good glass has a wide bowl which narrows towards the rim to keep the smell in (or bouquet if you prefer). This allows you to stick your nose in and get a good whiff.

Smell

All experts have their own set of jargon words, and wine experts and shippers have a particularly pretentious one. The 'nose' of a wine describes the way the wine smells and it is with the nose that you do most of your tasting (of food and drink). If you don't believe me, try tasting some wine with a clothes-peg on your nose, it will have no flavour! So, when you try a wine always have a good smell of it before you swallow, then invent your own language to shorthand its characteristic fragrances for future comparison. Most heavy red wines will benefit from being opened about an hour before you want to drink them to allow them to 'breathe' – this tends to improve the bouquet somewhat and hence makes them better to drink.

Alcohol

Swirl the wine in the (clean!) glass and then return the glass gently to the vertical. Hold the glass up to the light. You will see a transparent line where the surface of the wine touched the glass with 'legs' of moisture rather like the pillars of a church reaching back down to the surface of the wine. The length of these legs is in proportion to the strength of the wine. Try comparing Beaujolais with a heavy duty Rioja. (See, we don't only drink French wine!) So the next time you hear a Frenchman at a pavement café saying, '*Mon dieu, voyez ces jambes!*', it may be the wine and not Fifi Bon Chance with the pelmet skirt that has his attention. (Unlikely though.) Good, strong wines are like chorus girls; they have long legs.

Bubbles

Did you know that the British drink more fizz per head of population than anyone else in Europe, even the French? The main clue to the quality of Champagne and similar wines is the size, evenness, and speed of bubble production. The right stuff produces fairly large bubbles at an even rate for a long time. That's one of the reasons why we think that 'Lambretta' stuff (or is that a motor scooter? It is hard to tell!) is so awful.

Price

When you buy wine in this country the combination of shipping costs, Puritan taxation and the supplier's (comparatively) modest profits ensure that, in 1990, a £2.50 bottle may contain less than 50 odd pence worth of wine. It is amazing that it is as good as it is! However, as the taxes and shipping costs remain constant, and the margins don't change that much with price, it is easy to see that a £4.00 bottle has wine in it which is seven to eight times the value of the wine in a cheaper bottle. So paying a little more for your wine can bring a dramatic difference to the taste. This is particularly true of wines in the £3 to £10 range. After this you may be in the realms of diminishing returns – and debt!

Buying it	There are all kinds of outlets for wine – retailers such as Sainsbury's, Tesco, traditional off-licence chains like Oddbins, Peter Dominic and an ever-growing band of wholesalers, the best known being Majestic Wines. The key to these places is the people. Supermarkets have very expert buyers these days to ensure a good choice, but have minimal expertise to help you on the shop floor. Most off-licence chains train their staff, or at least their managers, so advice about the wines they stock should be available. Wholesalers offer the best combination of price and on the spot knowledge as well as making it possible to 'try before you buy'; they sometimes organise tasting evenings on wines from a particular region which can be very educational. *Caveat emptor*, beware the merchants who promote their wines with wine and cheese parties; there is a saying in the trade, 'Buy on an apple, sell on a cheese'. Try the experiment for yourself; cheese covers a multitude of sins in a poor wine and flatters the good; an apple ruins the best.
Temperature:	Nothing can kill a wine more quickly than drinking it at the wrong temperature. A cold red will be dull and flavourless, a warm white will be a total nonentity. Serious reds (Bordeaux, Burgundy, Côtes-du-Rhône, Rioja, Zinfandel, red port, etc.) should be served at room temperature, about 15° to 17°C/62°F, Beaujolais and similar light reds a little colder at about 11°C/52°F. Dry whites, such as Muscadet and rosé wines (try Clairet, the Bordeaux rosé) should be chilled to 9°C/48°F. Champagne, the real McCoy, at 9°C/48°F in an ice bucket, of course! And finally, the coldest of all, pudding (dessert) wines are served at a frosty 5°C/41°F.
With what and in what order?	The rule of thumb is white with fish or fowl, and red with meat and game. The 'weight' of the wine should match that of the food you serve it with. (Yes, that is the way round I meant.) Mild cheeses are easy, strong ones more difficult (hence port with Stilton), and

pudding wines go with sweet puddings (try a glass of Sauterne with a good Crème Brulée!). Also, never try to follow a heavy wine with a light one – it will just be wasted. You'll find a rough and ready guide to what goes with what at the end of this chapter.

Keeping wine

The biggest problem for most people is space. You need somewhere that has a fairly constant temperature (so the cupboard over the boiler is out) and is out of direct sunlight. The wine should be kept in racks (those cheap DIY wooden kits are ideal), horizontally in a place where it will not be disturbed too often. The cupboard with the ironing board and the vacuum cleaner is not a good bet. It should not be too hot (preferably less than 15°C/60°F) nor too cold (it should never freeze). The ideal temperature is about 11°C/52°F. Ideally it shouldn't be too damp or dry either. Life is never easy is it? What this means is that if you want to store wine for long periods of time (i.e. years) you need a proper cellar. Most of us don't have such a luxury and do the best we can. Our wine storage (for about sixty bottles) is the cupboard under the stairs. This is a good compromise, as although it does get a little hot in summer, the temperature does not change too rapidly and the wine doesn't get disturbed too often. We don't buy wine that needs to be kept more than two or three years, and we only have a few bottles in that category for future special occasions.

The next thing is what to keep. This depends on space.

A basic cellar: most people only have space for a few dozen bottles of wine, and unless you have a lot of space you should think of your cellar as a store of drinkables. Don't worry about laying down wine; simply think about what you will need to go with most meals. As a guide, here is a list of what we think you might keep in a cellar of twenty-four bottles.

3 Bottles   Bordeaux red
3 Bottles   Burgundy
6 Bottles   Loire White
3 Bottles   Alsace White
2 Bottles   Dessert Wine
3 Bottles   Beaujolais
2 Bottles   Champagne (Keep in the fridge?)
2 Bottles   Rioja

This is, of course, a fairly arbitrary selection and the system is that you top it up once it gets down to half full. The idea behind it is to provide a suitable accompaniment to most of the meals that you are likely to serve up. You should keep a record of the wine that you use. You may find that you use a lot more of one sort than another and you can adjust your stock levels accordingly. Always choose wines that suit your own tastes, not what you expect others to like, and keep trying new wines from time to time.

If you have more space, you might start keeping some wine for the future, and having a wider range of wines in different categories. You can have a lot of fun 'growing' a cellar of your own.

To give you a few ideas, we've provided some notes on the types of wine that we buy. It is by no means a comprehensive selection and leaves out a lot of wine-producing regions. But we've not had any complaints about the wine yet and some of our friends are definitely not too polite to complain!

French Wines

Hint: As a rough and ready guarantee of quality, the AC (*Appellation Controlée*) system which applies to about a sixth of all French wine, provides some idea of what you're going to get. It specifies the region, the grape and how it is made. You will know what you are getting.

Red

Beaujolais Everyone knows Beaujolais, if only because all the wine bars go mad every November with 'The *Nouveau Beaujolais est arrivé*' chalked up all over the place. Whether you like Beaujolais Nouveau or not (the French ignore it, and we're not that smitten with the stuff), the wines from this region are well worth drinking. Made from Gamay grapes, these wines are full of fruit and very fresh. They are designed to be drunk when they are young, and they are light enough to be consumed freely. Drink them just slightly chilled. Beaujolais-Villages is a more up-market version, with la crème de la crème being the 'Crus Beaujolais' such as Fleurie, Brouilly and Juliénas (to name but three of the ten).

Bordeaux This region was effectively British from AD 1154, then the French regained it in 1453 when the Earl of Shrewsbury (Henry VI was on the throne at the time) lost the battle of Castillon. In my opinion this is one of the greatest military disasters in the history of Great Britain. I think we should have offered them Cornwall in part exchange. However it is still one of the most Anglophilic parts of France, and if you've never been to France, it is one of the best parts to start with. So much for the history lesson; back to the wine. *Toujours les vins*. In case you haven't guessed, this is our favourite region. The wines are usually made from Cabernet Sauvignon (50 per cent), Merlot (20 per cent), and Cabernet Franc (10 per cent) grapes, with the remainder from Malbec and Petit Verdot. The mix varies considerably throughout the region. Some wines are pure Cabernet Sauvignon and St Emilion wines contain significantly more Merlot than anything else. This means that you can enjoy a tremendous variation in red Bordeaux. The main areas are Côtes de Bourg, Entre-Deux-Mers, Fronsac, Graves, Médoc, Pomerol, Premier Côte de

Bordeaux, and St Emilion. The most expensive wines come from Médoc, St Emilion and Pomerol. We have a running battle over which are better – the wines from around Margaux in the Médoc (wines which tell you what to do, but the message is worth hearing) or from St Emilion (wines with which you can have a conversation) – now there's pretension for you! Down to earth. Bordeaux reds have more tannin than other French reds and this is what gives them their distinctive Claret quality. They are often wines that need to be kept if they are to be enjoyed at their best – this is more true of the Médoc wines than the softer St Emilion wines. All are strong (12 per cent and above) and should have a good colour. Incidentally many warehouses and supermarkets stock generic Bordeaux wines, e.g. Margaux (not Château Margaux or there'd be an extra nought or two on the price), St Emilion, St Estèphe, Médoc and so on. These are made from surplus wine from the main producers and are often extremely good value. Incidentally the reason the British call it Claret is because in olden times (Henry II) they used to ship large quantities of Clairet, a pale red, almost rosé, wine to England. You can still get it; it makes a nice summer drink.

Burgundy

There are many people who maintain that the best red wines in the world come from Burgundy. That may be debatable but there are certainly magnificent wines to be had here. The red Burgundy wines are variable, but they make for easier drinking than Bordeaux. Their character is more immediate than Claret, they aren't backward in being forward. As a rule they don't last as long and are ready to be drunk much earlier. Unfortunately the region only produces about a tenth as much wine as Bordeaux, consequently it tends to be more expensive. They are made from the Pinot Noir grape, though some of the non-*Appellation Controlée* wines use the Gamay grape as well. In ascending order of quality Burgundy wines are defined as: Bourgogne Grande Ordinaire, Bourgogne AC (*Appellation Controlée*), Côte de Beaune Villages, Côte de Nuits Villages, the commune wines with names that include Givry and Mercurey, then it's onwards and upwards through such things as Gevrey-Chambertin until your bank manager objects. In our view the best Burgundy wines are overpriced mainly because of shortage of supply and popularity in the American markets. However, they are excellent wines and are extremely pleasant accompaniments to rich meals.

Buying old Burgundy can be a risky business; don't do it without good advice unless you are an expert yourself.

Loire

They do make some red wine here. It is made from the Cabernet Franc grape that is also used in small percentages in some Bordeaux wines. The best known (to us, at any rate) is Chinon. The wines are fruity and dry and not too alcoholic. Like Beaujolais they benefit from being drunk slightly cooler than most reds. Drink young.

Rhône

This is a generic name for wines made in the Rhône valley, south of Lyons. There are two distinct halves to the region, north and south. The wines from the north (Hermitage) are heavyweight stuff and need to be kept for quite a long time before they are ready to drink. The wines from the south, which includes most of the Côtes du Rhône and Châteauneuf-du-Pape, are easier going and can be drunk earlier. Côtes du Rhône typically has 11 per cent alcohol and should be drunk young. Côtes du Rhône-Villages is a stronger (12.5 per cent) and more complicated version which needs to be kept a while if it's going to be enjoyed.

Châteauneuf-du-Pape, a very complicated wine, uses over a dozen different grape varieties in the region. It is powerful (12.5 per cent) and full of bite and has been described as a 'casserole in a bottle' and improves with keeping. It is really good to drink with roast beef and all the trimmings on a winter's day.

White

Alsace

These wines are made from German grapes, but they are produced using French methods, so you get the best of both worlds. The wines have a delightful flowery smell to them but have a nice dryness once you have them in your mouth. The most popular one is the Gewürtztraminer, well known for its difficulty in spelling and pronunciation. These wines are very nice to drink on their own on a summer's evening; they make a very good apéritif. Because they are not among the most popular, these wines can often be found at attractive prices. However, you should be warned that they are a lot more alcoholic than their German equivalents.

Bordeaux

You get both sweet and dry whites from here. What's more they come in a tremendous range of price and quality (not always related!). Arguably the best pudding wines in the world, Sauternes and Barsac, come from here. (Château Yquem is justly prized, and justly pricey.) For a cheap alternative to these expensive dessert wines try a sweet Graves or Premier Côte de Bordeaux wine. Dry white from Graves and Entre-Deux-Mers should be considered as an alternative to Loire whites.

Burgundy

The best Burgundy whites are produced from the Chardonnay grape. The wines are dry, rich and complex. The better ones will mature for over ten years. The most famous wines of this type are the Chablis wines which come in three categories (in increasing price): Chablis, Premier Cru, and Grand Cru. The latter wines can be frighteningly expensive – have them for special occasions. All Chablis wines have lots of flavour and a very nice gold colour.

Champagne

Charlie knew what he was about; there really is no better game than this. Apart from the bubbles, choosing Champagne is the same as choosing any other wine; colour, smell and so on. It comes in varying degrees of dryness (or sweetness, if you want to look at it that way). However, most people seem to like the dry (Brut) sort best. There is considerable controversy about pink champagne. Some think it the Bees' Roller Skates, others think it an abomination. Make up your own mind. Vintage is better than non-vintage and it is reflected in the price but it is worth the extra, unless you're going to add Crème de Cassis to make a Kir Royale, that is.

Loire

This region is known for its crisp dry white wines, Muscadet being the most famous, Sancerre and Pouilly Fumé being the most expensive. The wines should be drunk when young and cold (the wines, not you). Buying Muscadet can be complicated – it comes in three varieties: Muscadet is a simple, sharp dry wine, Muscadet de Sèvre-et-Maine (tributaries to the Loire) is a more prestigious wine with a bit more to it, and 'sur-lie' means that they bottled it straight off the lees and should have more flavour. You expect them to be priced accordingly, though no Muscadet wine is very expensive.

Italian Wines

The Italians make extremely good drinking wine; they are much easier to get on with for everyday quaffing than the great French wines. This doesn't mean that there are not some outstanding Italian wines. There are, but it's the tippling wine that we know best.

Hint: The Italian equivalent to the French AC system is the DOC (*Denominazione d'Origine Controllata*).

Unfortunately, Italian bureaucracy being what it is, this has not worked out too well and you will find many wines that are called *vino da tavola* which are better. However, that's the only clue you're going to get.

Red

Barola and Barbaresco — These are neighbouring wines from south of Turin. They are strong (13 per cent), full of fruit, full of life and have potential for ageing. These are much tougher than the average Italian red and have to be taken seriously. They should be at least five years old before you drink them.

Bardolino — A light red wine which has a pale colour. It is a good wine to serve to people who are not regular drinkers. Drink young.

Chianti — This must be the most famous red wine from Italy. It comes from Florence and has lots of fruit and is full of life. Some Chianti ages very well, but most can be drunk when it is three- to four-years-old. There is a superior Classico version available. A medium-weight wine.

Valpolicella — They make an awful lot of this stuff if the supermarket shelves are anything to go by. It is a lightweight red wine, like Bardolino, and should be similarly treated. You are strongly advised to avoid the litre and larger bottles (even more so the wine-box varieties).

White

Frascati — Very well known and very popular, it comes from the Roman hills and is dry with a good yellow colour. It tastes of grapes (how odd!) and is served cold. One of the better versions is Fontana Candida. Drink young.

Marsala	This is made the same way as Sherry. It is strong, dark and can be sweet or dry. The primary ingredient of Zabaglione, one of Italy's best puddings, it can be taken as a dessert wine or as an apéritif.
Soave	About the best known of all Italian wines. We're willing to bet that a lot of young ladies have been led astray after a few glasses of this in their formative years. It is fresh and dry (again serve chilled) and usually unexceptional. Steer clear of extra large bottles and wine boxes. Does not age – drink young.
Asti Spumante	This is a muscat-based (and consequently sweet) sparkling wine. It has a low alcohol content and is thus ideal for parties which include hordes of adolescents. Often served at weddings.
Spanish Wines	These are well established with the British drinking public, especially the Riojas. White wines should not be more than one- or two-years-old when drunk, though some white Riojas get 'oakier' with age and are exceptions to this guideline. The red Riojas are very like the Bordeaux wines of France, but a little cheaper (and made from a different grape, of course). The wines from the Navarra region are growing in popularity and are well worth trying; they tend to be a little cheaper than Riojas.
German Wines	German wines are often sneered at by the wine-buying public. This is largely the Germans' own fault for producing a lot of sweet, watery, wine-box, featureless plonk, most of which is not even suitable for making into punch. Consequently German wines tend to be very reasonably priced. This is a good thing for drinkers, as there are some very good German wines available, with an increasing amount of *trocken* (dry) wines which are good to drink with food. These wines are much more like those from the Alsace area in France. Hint: Hocks come in brown bottles and Moselle wines in green bottles.

Hint: The German *Qualitätswein* means that the wine has met the most minimal of standards – don't expect it to be much of a guarantee.

English Wines These are similar to the better German wines in style (but not in price; they tend to be expensive). However they do need to be kept longer than German wines prior to drinking, four years or more depending on the wine. They are almost invariably white wines. A word of warning, do not confuse them with 'British Wines'. In our opinion these blended concoctions are not to be recommended.

American Wines For many people this implies Californian in general and Napa Valley in particular. This is rather unfair on the rest of California and the rest of the States, but for the casual buyer it makes life a lot easier. You can get everything from heavy-duty Cabernet Sauvignon Bordeaux-style reds to sharp dry Loire-style whites. American wines tend to have much more interesting names than those from anywhere else: Firestone (makes you tired if you have too much) and Zinfandel Blush (a shy little wine?). The former is a serious red wine of Bordeaux style, the latter is a fashionable apéritif wine (not too alcoholic).

Australian Wines These have recently become more popular as the quality of wines available in this country has increased markedly over the last few years. The full range of wines are available from dry whites to full-bodied reds. We have become very fond of a wine with the unlikely name of Glenloth. It compares very favourably with Bordeaux wines costing twice the price.

Party Game

For those who are wine enthusiasts, try playing Desert Island Wines. Choose the eight bottles that you would take with you to your desert island.

Here is our wining and dining checklist:

Buying	What advice do you need? This depends on how expert you are. Do you get a discount for buying by the case? Can you buy mixed cases? Essential if you have limited storage. Will they deliver? Can you try before you buy? Are they helpful and knowledgeable?
Keeping	Is the temperature even? Will the wine be disturbed often? Can you get at the wine easily? Is it away from sunlight?
Serving	Have you updated the wine book? Is the wine at the right temperature? Does it go with the food? Is it the right type of glass? Has it been left to breathe?

What Goes with What?

Apéritif	Try any of the following (though not all at once, unless you want to have a cocktail party instead of a meal, in which case cut down on the food): Sherry, White Port (Chilled), Dry White Wine, Champagne, Gewürztraminer, all go well with ordinary nibblies. For a change, try a sweet wine served with pâté de foie, this Bordelaise tradition is delightful. Do not serve peanuts – they don't go well with wine.
Soups	These are often too strong to drink wine with, so either have them *sans vino* or perhaps with a little sherry.
Smoked salmon	Alsace, Chablis or Champagne. If served with scrambled eggs for breakfast, then definitely Champagne, preferably vintage.

Pasta	This depends entirely on the sauce. Meat and tomato-based sauces imply red wines; fish and vegetable based sauces imply white wine. We think you should stick to Italian wine with Pasta, but it isn't essential.
Fish	Most fish demands that you serve a white wine, the dryness of the wine being dependent on the nature of the fish. You might find that some of the stronger-tasting fish may merit a light red.
Shellfish	Dry and white, for a tasty bite!
Meat	As a rule, red to match the blood! (Sorry, Vegetarians.) Pork will go with either red or white, but the wine should be fairly rich, not a Muscadet, more of a Chablis. Roast beef goes wonderfully with a good red Burgundy or a St Emilion. If you're having a rich sauce, then choose a wine that can cope with it.
Barbecued meat	The strength of the sauces and marinades makes this a bit tricky. But a cheap but oomphy red is a good idea, possibly a Chianti or a Rioja.
Poultry	The general rule is a not too dry white but we have found that you can drink pretty much what you like as long as you keep a balance between the wine and any sauce you make. After all, Coq au Vin is made with red Burgundy.
Game	This is easy. A good red wine is the perfect complement to Roast Pheasant, Grouse, Guinea Fowl, Venison, etc. Err on the side of strength and complexity: Châteauneuf-du-Pape, St Emilion, Gevrey Chambertin and so forth.
Curry	Difficult. Lager louts have it aright. Indian beer is best. But if you insist on having wine, try a German white.

Vegetarian	It is sad but vegetarian food does not lend itself very well to wine. Perhaps one of the organically produced wines would be a safe bet, and dry whites seem to be the closest match to the flavours of a vegetable casserole.
Cheese	Wine goes superbly well with cheese, hence the wine and cheese parties of old. Medical researchers have even shown that the alcohol helps to break down the cholesterol from the cheese, so you can almost call it healthy eating. Having said all that, it can be tricky to get it exactly right. Mild cheeses such as Cheddar go with most red wines and can be safely combined with a quality Burgundy or Bordeaux to the benefit of both. Strong cheeses need a sweet wine of some kind if the wine isn't going to be humiliated. The classic examples being Port and Stilton, Sauterne and Roquefort. Cream cheeses such as Brie and Camembert are best suited with a reasonably heavy wine – we prefer red. Hint: Try a cheese from the same region as the wine (or vice versa), for example, St Estèphe with a St Estèphe wine.
Dessert	Ice cream and sorbets should be taken neat. Other puddings, which tend to be sweet, should have an even sweeter wine: Sauterne, Barsac, the ubiquitous Muscat de Beaumes-de-Venise, Marsala and so on. Don't serve wine with fruit salad; it will taste awful. Put some in the fruit salad instead.

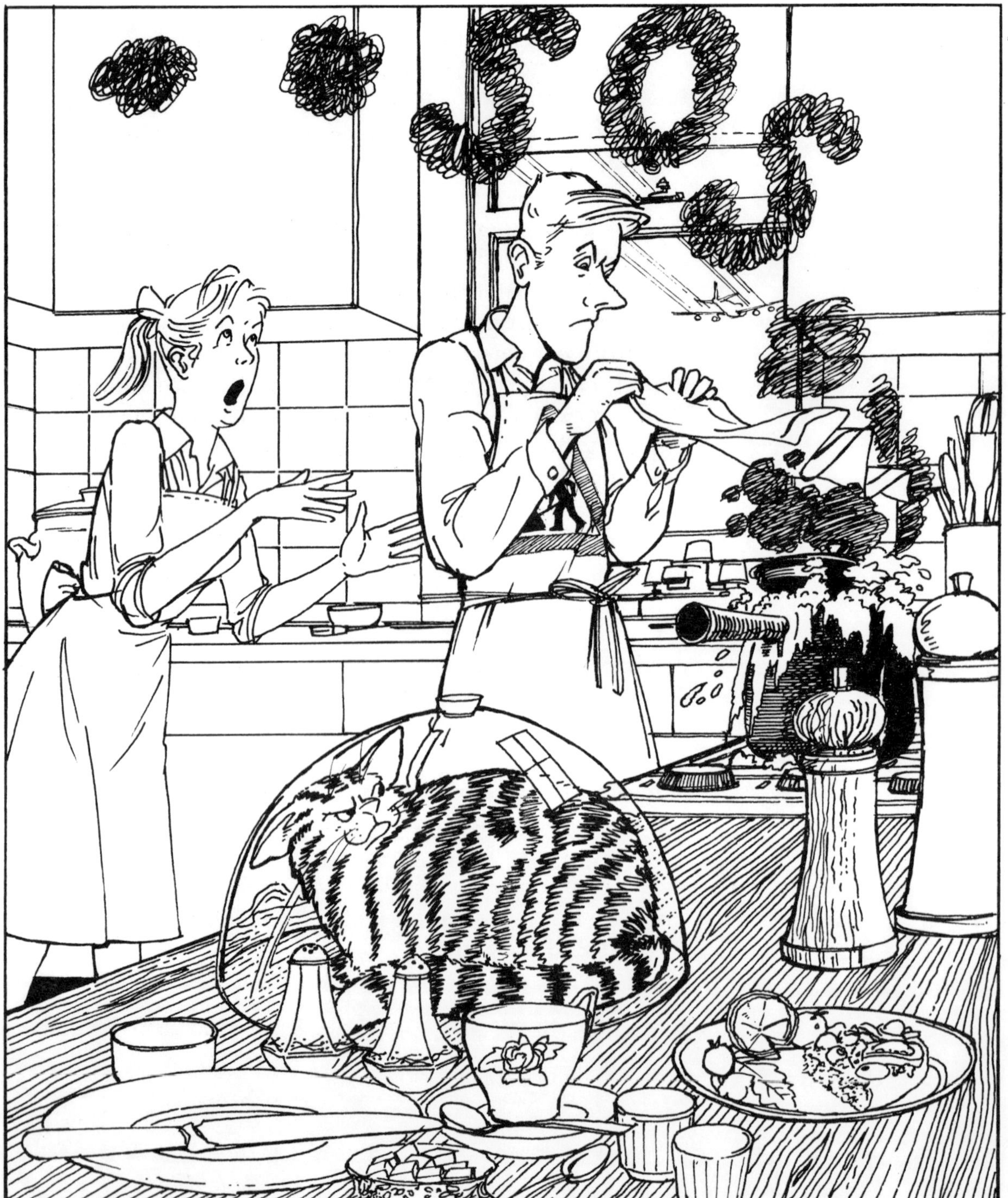

Chapter 4

Two People, One Kitchen
or
I Told You I'd Left the Stock on the Gas

> **Manoeuvr/e², *-euver, v.i. & t.**
>
> **Perform, cause (troops) to perform, manoeuvres; employ artifice; force, drive (person, thing *out*, *into*, *away*, etc.) by contrivance; manipulate adroitly; n. deceptive or elusive movement; skilful plan. [L. *manu operare* to work by hand]**

You've got the kitchen sorted out, you've worked out what you're going to cook and you have the provisions to make it with. You've even got plenty of wine. But now you've got to cook together, in the same kitchen! At the same time! This is the ultimate test of any relationship.

We have identified three Cs for success – Communication, Compromise and Clearing-Up-As-You-Go-Along.

Communication You really do have to let each other know what is going on. Our classic example of miscommunication went like this. I had made up a plate of smoked salmon with dill sauce ready for the first course. Because the cats are somewhat keen on this starter (or, to be honest, almost any food that is going) I put it on top of a wall cupboard, the one that has the wine glasses in it. I then popped out to make sure that the guests were all

(It was the dill sauce that was the real problem – that and the bruising. – S.)

suitably plied with beverages, and that none of them had been savaged by a hungry cat or one of the other guests. As I returned to the kitchen I was just in time to see the plate of smoked salmon fall on Suzy's head. Since Suzy had not been told about the unusual resting place for the salmon, she had opened the cupboard causing the fishy downpour. I'd assumed that as the glasses were already on the table no risk was involved.

Another example was a stockpot we both thought the other was looking after, making sure it didn't boil dry and so on. Unfortunately the first we knew about it was an interesting smell. We were able to turn off the gas, allow it to cool a bit and add water before there was an actual fire, but we now think we know what witches smelt like when they were burnt. It took four days before the smell cleared and about three hours to resurrect the stockpot. *Communicate!*

Compromise

The way that you split the work up between you will also make a huge difference to how well you're going to get on in the kitchen. If you like, it can be seen as an extension of the planning you did before you got this far. (You did do the planning, didn't you?) This is where the next C comes in. Compromise. There are three different ways of splitting the work up. There's the Master/Slave system, the First Among Equals system, and the You-Wash-And-I'll-Dry system.

1 The Master/Slave approach

This is fine if one of you is a kitchen wimp, when it will work very well indeed. One person (who knows what he or she is doing) is the boss. The other one does as he or she is told, e.g. peeling the potatoes, washing the pans and generally having a miserable time. If you find that this works for you then we think you ought to reconsider the nature of your relationship.

2 The First Among Equals

If you both have reasonable skills then this can be a real winner. You each take charge of different aspects of the meal, i.e. one person cooks the main course, the other cooks the guz-before and the guz-after. You then support your partner when they are centre stage in the kitchen. In effect, there is only one person in charge at any given time. On average you will get a fairly even mix of pleasant and unpleasant jobs, at least over a number of meals. You also get to share the prestige.

3 You-Wash-And-I'll-Dry

This is the most cooperative approach. Nobody is in charge, and both of you have an equal involvement in every job that has to be done. This is something of a culinary Utopia. We've never been able to make this one work, preferring the First Among Equals method. Unless you are very easy-going and almost totally without ego, this approach is not for you.

Whichever method you choose there are several areas where disagreements will occur, the first one being the cooker/oven/hob.

We have several basic rules about this:

* Never allow the handles of any pans on the cooker to stick out into the working space. Keep all handles pointing as far as possible towards the back of the cooker. But watch out that they don't get burnt/melted.

* If you need to cook several vegetables at once, use a stacking steamer pan.

* If the oven needs to be really hot for the meat course (for a roast or grill for example), then choose a pudding that does not need cooking in the oven.

* If you are frying food, try to keep a lid on the frying pan. If this is not possible (steak, for example, which needs watching carefully), then only one person should be near the cooker. The fryer *immediately* wipes down the hob when finished.

* All roasting pans to be soaked in hot soapy water as soon as possible.

* The person making the velvety smooth custard or sauce or gravy is king or queen of the cooker and is *never* interrupted.

Hint: Electric rings need more managing than gas rings because of the time that it takes them to heat up and cool down (**NB**: this does not apply to halogen type electric rings). This is especially important when you have two people using the same hob; they will invariably spend their time turning up/down each other's pans. What you can do is have one of the rings on high (turn it on a little before you need it) two on medium and one on low or off. You then move the pans from one to the other when required. This saves having to wait while rings change temperature. You can then make fine adjustments to temperature as required. This system is even more flexible if you have somewhere to stand a pan by the hob, effectively freeing the fourth ring. If this seems too much trouble, then get a gas/halogen hob.

From fire to water – the next minefield is the sink.

In a perfect world, the sink should be clear at all times unless it is actually being used. We have had more rows about the state of the dishcloth and the lack of room on the draining board than almost anything else.

(Usually wet, slightly slimy and lurking at the bottom of the bowl – if David has been at it. – S.)

Here are our rules:

* No knives left in the water.

* All mixing bowls and mixing implements to be washed, dried and put back into storage or where they will be needed *immediately after use*.

* Draining board to be kept clear.

* Soaking of roasting pans does not take place until the sink is not needed for a considerable length of time (e.g. during the meal).

* Dishcloth to be *wrung out* thoroughly after use!

This brings us on neatly to the third C.

Clearing Up

Clear up as you go along. This is crucial; it makes the difference between having a clean and efficient working environment and all-out nuclear war.

Clearing up isn't just a matter of washing up the used utensils; it covers putting things away, keeping the working surfaces clean, changing the rubbish bag when it's full, keeping the chopping boards clean and accessible . . .

(and putting the butter back into the fridge, not leaving it to melt over the working surfaces. – S.)

This is the general procedure we use:

Choose your working areas.

Put away anything that you are not going to need and make as much clear space as possible.

Get out anything you are going to need and arrange it in the order you are going to use it.

Check that you have spare rubbish bags, paper towels, drying cloths.

Make space in the fridge if you need to chill anything.

Designate the spaces to be used for cooling cakes, bread, pastries, etc., 'resting' cooked joints or defrosting frozen foods and try to keep these areas away from the main activity.

(and the cats/children/dogs. – S.)

The one who needs the oven first, takes priority.

When you are between tasks – lay the table, check the drinks, chase the cats out of the kitchen, put out the ashtrays, deadhead the flowers, decant the ice cubes into a bowl and keep them in the fridge, cut up the lemons, prepare the cocktails, lay out the nibblies, chase the cats away from the nibblies, choose the music, check the bathroom for spare towels and chase the cats away from the nibblies again.

And always remember the 3 Cs. Communicate, Compromise and Clear Up as you go along.

Here's a checklist:

Communicate	Have you told each other what you think is happening?
Have you told them where you put it?

Compromise	How are you going to work together?
What are the 'rules of the kitchen'?

Clear Up	Are you clearing up as you go along?

> "Let us have wine and women, mirth and laughter,
> Sermons and soda-water the day after"
> *Byron*

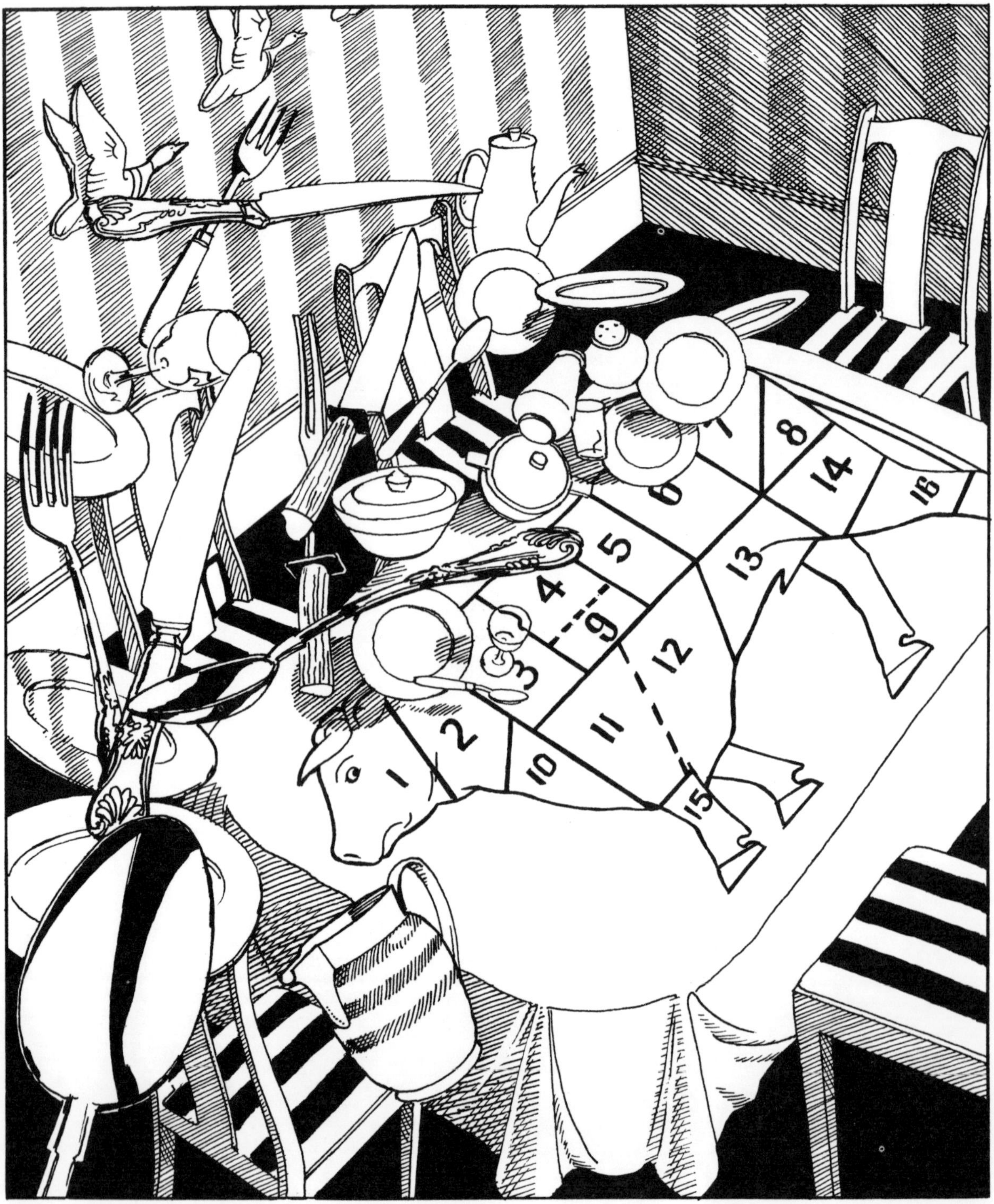
1
2
3
4
5
6
7
8
9
10
11
12
13
14
15
16

Chapter 5

Serving It Up
or
You Cut and I'll Deal
or
The Speed of the Hand Deceives the Fly

> **How you serve the meal can make a major difference to the success of the occasion. Scamper about in all directions, rush people from course to course, give an impression of chaos and everyone is going to be just a smidge tense.**
>
> **Before even the first course hoves into view your guests will be making a judgement on the cooking. This is because they can see how you have laid the table. The table provides the stage upon which the food struts its stuff. You have to strike a balance between appearance and functionality.**

Table Layout

A critical factor in this will be the size of the table and the number of guests. When you have a small table and as many guests as can sit round it, you are well advised to serve up the meal in the kitchen and restrict the table to place settings only.

If you have a small table and a great number of guests then a buffet supper is the answer, where the table is used as a refuelling centre and the guests eat in the living room.

Setting the table for a sit-down meal

To make life easy for everyone and to give an attractive layout, simply place the individual cutlery on either side of the place mat; knives and spoons on the right, forks on the left. The rule is work from the outside in; this should include the dessertspoons and forks as well. Wine glasses go on the right of the settings, and if more than one wine is being served then the glasses should be arranged in order of the wines to be served, the nearest glass for the first wine and so on.

Side plates and napkins go to the left of the place setting.

Cutlery

This is largely a matter of personal taste, though classical designs in stainless steel are very practical and attractive for both everyday and formal use. Even if you are buying expensive cutlery you may consider having the knife blades in stainless steel on the grounds of sharpness and durability. If there is any doubt about the continued availability of the cutlery, then buy an extra place setting to allow for losses (a teaspoon in the garbage disposal is not a retrievable item).

As a minimum, each place setting should include a large and small knife, large and small fork, dessertspoon, soup spoon and a teaspoon. We find that four serving spoons are needed, and have collected a selection of gravy ladles, soup ladles and assorted pickle forks, spoons and salad servers that we use when necessary. Fish knives and forks are still considered to be *de trop*.

Glassware

One of the great beauties of a wine is its colour. The reds of Burgundy and the Sauternes of Bordeaux have colours which would do credit to a medieval stained-glass window. So the glasses you use should show this off. They should also enhance the aroma of the wine. This means that the majority of those cut-glass jobs are right out, sorry about that. The ideal is thin-walled, undecorated, tulip-shaped, and made of high quality glass. They are easily obtained and can be bought in different sizes to suit red wine, white wine, Champagne and dessert wines. A set of matching tumblers for mineral water or soft drinks will complete the collection.

Dinner services and crockery

As with glassware for the wine, the china is there for the benefit of the food. Complicated, garishly patterned tableware does not show food at its best. It is no fun to have the *Rape of the Sabine Women* looming up at you beneath your consommé. If you do want decorated tableware then try to get a range which has the pattern round the edge and a plain or white centre for the food to be displayed on. We actually use three sets of crockery. An old Denbyware four-place setting we call our 'Family' crockery. We use this when we're on our own, or with people who we know very well. This total lack of ceremony and the informality is for people who form our extended family.

(This is really sturdy crockery and can be bashed around in the kitchen, used to store leftover food on in the fridge and has (so far) withstood all my efforts to break it – something I cannot claim for the finer stuff. – S.)

We have a plain blue and white patterned dishwasher-proof eight-place setting in bone china which we use for most ordinary dinner parties and lunches. It is a mass-produced item and so is easy to replace if broken and can be washed with abandon. It is smart and practical and food looks well on it. We also have a bone china non-dishwasher set for 'best'; this is used when we want to impress, or (more often) when we want to celebrate something, like getting paid by a publisher.

(Since I have broken three pieces so far, we need a new contract each time we use it! – S.)

(We have seen this idea used most effectively where not only did each guest have a different place setting, but also a matching napkin, set of glasses and tiny flower arrangement. The tablecloth, candlesticks and candles were white and so were all the serving dishes – it looked marvellous. – S.)

An alternative to having a matched dinner service is to buy individual place settings so that everyone has their own unique service for the meal. This also allows you to buy the highest quality in odds and ends at a substantial saving. You can then choose the service that you think is most appropriate for each guest.

Serving the Food

Serving dishes can be phenomenally expensive; the covered vegetable dishes that go with our 'best' china cost the equivalent of a set of new car tyres! As an alternative you could use stainless steel dishes – we have one with five compartments which takes all the vegetables and looks very decorative in the centre of the table. Serving dishes should be warmed before use (unless of course you are serving salad) so that the food stays hot while they are being passed around. Have a spare napkin handy for holding them if the handles are too hot to hold for long.

If you are serving up in the kitchen then the only thing that need concern you is arranging the food carefully on the plates and having hot plates for hot food ready to take in to the guests. This allows everyone to be served at the same time with each course, thus avoiding the business of waiting for the host and hostess to be served whilst your guests' food goes cold. In these days of equality it is not always necessary to serve the ladies first. However, we still do, and if challenged will justify it on the grounds of positive discrimination.

Arranging the food on the plate

The best thing that *nouvelle cuisine* (and, in our opinion the only thing) did for cooking was to make the presentation of the food a work of art: pictures made of food on the plates. It doesn't make any difference to how the food tastes, but it makes a big difference to people's expectations. If people are serving themselves, then this is not quite as relevant, except that you can always make a dish of new potatoes look that much better with the addition of a sprig of mint and a dab of melting butter. However, when you set out the food on a plate there are some things worth thinking about. How do the colours go together? Should the meal look symmetrical, or perhaps the meat should be on one side, the vegetables on the other? If there is a sauce, where on the plate should it be poured? It is all a matter of opinion, but you can usually tell when it looks right, and a few minutes' thought before you serve is amply rewarded. People will think you have spent a lot more time than you actually have, which is most gratifying. It is also wise to consider whether fancy arrangements are appropriate to the meal – sausage casserole and mashed potato should be dolloped not sculpted.

(Our proof reader hated the word 'prettifying'. So did I; we prefer tarting up! – D.)

Here are some ideas for decorating and prettifying simple food:

Chopped herbs on almost everything from fish, to meat, to vegetables.

A tiny bouquet of mint leaves, dill fronds and chives, watercress or any other seasonal herbs (check the mix of the flavours first).

A spiral of cream poured over the back of a teaspoon into the centre of a bowl of soup.

Croutons scattered over soup just before serving.

Thinly cut circles of cucumber arranged in a pattern on top of the soup or around one side of a plate.

Vegetables such as mangetout, haricot beans, tiny carrots or baby sweetcorn fanned out around the meat.

Thinly cut orange or lemon slices.

Slivered and toasted almonds scattered over vegetables such as broccoli, beans or Brussels sprouts.

Small, feathery green leaves from the centre of a head of celery arranged by the meat.

Borage flowers strewn over a fruity pudding.

Carefully and thinly sliced fresh fruit such as strawberries, passion fruit, kiwi fruit or star fruit arranged in a pattern on one side of the plate.

Tiny, fresh flower heads arranged round the edge of a pudding plate. (Make sure they are edible!)

Carving

(I do the carving in our house, probably because I'm the only one with a decent carving knife and I won't let anyone else use it. This is how I handle the different cuts of meat. – S.)

Don't carve at table unless you can do it well. It's better to carve in the privacy of the kitchen and give the mistakes to the cat. Then you can fan the slices of meat out onto a large platter and serve from that.

Sharpen all knives before any carving takes place.

You will need your favourite carving knife and sometimes a little, slender, pointed and very sharp knife for freeing meat from the bones. Use a carving fork with a carving guard that flips up to protect your fingers.

If possible, use a carving dish with spikes in its base to anchor the meat and put a tea towel under the carving dish so that the dish doesn't slide about on the work surface.

Have a thoroughly warmed plate by the carving dish ready to take the carved meat.

Now to the surgery . . .
If the meat has been chined before cooking (see Chapter 2), remove the bones.

PORK LOIN — Remove the crackling and carve it into strips. Using a sharp little knife, free the curved rib bones from the meat. Now cut the meat up across the grain as if you were slicing up a sandwich loaf. If you don't want to bother with the removal of the rib bones, you can cut the roast pork into chops by cutting between the ribs, but this is not nearly as nice as thinner slices. Rolled, Boned Pork Shoulder is treated very much the same except that there are no bones to remove.

PORK LEG — Remove the crackling as before, now carve the meat in slices, starting at the broad, blunt end and carving round the bone. Every three or so slices, turn the joint over and carve from the other side.

BEST END OF LAMB	Cut this into chops and serve two or three to each person.
LEG OF LAMB	Traditionally this is carved from the middle (half way between the pointed end and the blunt end) by first making a central cut across the grain and down to the bone and then making a slightly slanted cut towards the first one, again down to the bone and lifting the slice of meat free. You carry on slicing on each side of the central V-shaped cut until you run out of meat. Personally I find this too fiddly so I treat leg of lamb just like a leg of pork, slicing across the blunt end and round the bone, carving slices off until you get to the lovely knobby bits at the pointed end (I usually sneak a few of these in the kitchen when I'm carving and tell David I gave them to the cats).
SHOULDER OF LAMB	This has so many angles that it can look daunting. I carve from the top side (the convex side with the fat on) slanting the knife blade so that it cuts across rather than along the grain of the meat, moving the joint about so that I can get as much off as possible, then turn the joint over and do much the same thing to the underside. There will be several knobby bits left, so use a small knife and carve as much off as you can.
BEEF	My favourite beef joint is Rib of Beef. This is the really tender eye of the meat, still on the bone. It cooks easily, is amazingly tasty but is quite difficult to carve unless you buy a really enormous piece. Because of this, smaller rib of beef joints are often boned and rolled by the butcher before they are cooked. Even if you buy the meat on the bone, ask the butcher to truss it for you as the trussing strings keep the eye of the meat and the outer layer together while carving.
	To carve rib of beef on the bone, place the rib joint flat on its side on a large dish (preferably a carving dish

with anchor spikes on its base) and sharpen up your carving knife to razor sharpness. Do not remove the trussing strings – these will keep the meat together and are easy to remove once the meat is sliced. Steady the meat with the carving fork making sure that the guard (the little prong on the front of the carving fork) is up; now start to carve from the fatty side of the meat towards the rib bone, cutting across the grain of the beef. The first few slices will be easy as the meat stands slightly proud of the bone, but as you get to the level of the bone you will need to use shorter carving strokes and angle the blade slightly down. When the knife gets to the bone, gently free the slice with the tip of the knife.

Most other beef joints are sold boned and rolled and are carved across the grain like a loaf of bread.

When carving beef a fair amount of the meat juices squeeze out of the meat onto the carving dish. Occasionally you should pour these into the gravy to add to the flavour.

CHICKENS, TURKEYS, GUINEA FOWL, GROUSE, PHEASANTS

These are usually trussed for roasting and the trussing strings need to be removed before carving. If the bird has been stuffed, spoon out the stuffing from the cavity before carving and keep warm until it is needed.

All birds need to be thoroughly cooked, not just because of any worries about salmonella or other food poisoning but also because they taste terrible if undercooked and are extremely difficult to carve. To tell if a bird is done, wiggle one leg; it should move easily and when you peer into the angle between the leg and the breast, there should be no pinkness or blood showing. If the leg does not move easily return the bird to the oven (covering the breast with foil to stop it drying out) and cook until it passes the wiggle test.

Carving: Wiggle the leg (you may need to slice through the skin between the leg and the body to do this) until you can poke the tip of the carving knife into the 'shoulder' joint between the two bones of the joint. You then slice cleanly through the joint to detach it from the body. Do the same with the other leg. Now wiggle the shoulder joint where one wing joins the body, slice through a little of the breast until you can feel the joint of the wing and detach as before. Do the same with the other wing. You now have a limbless fowl that will be easy to carve up into neat slices, carving downwards from the breastbone on one side and then on the other. Finally, turn the bird on its side and scoop out the tender 'oysters' of meat in the little hollows just behind where the wing joints joined the body. Save the carcass and make stock from it.

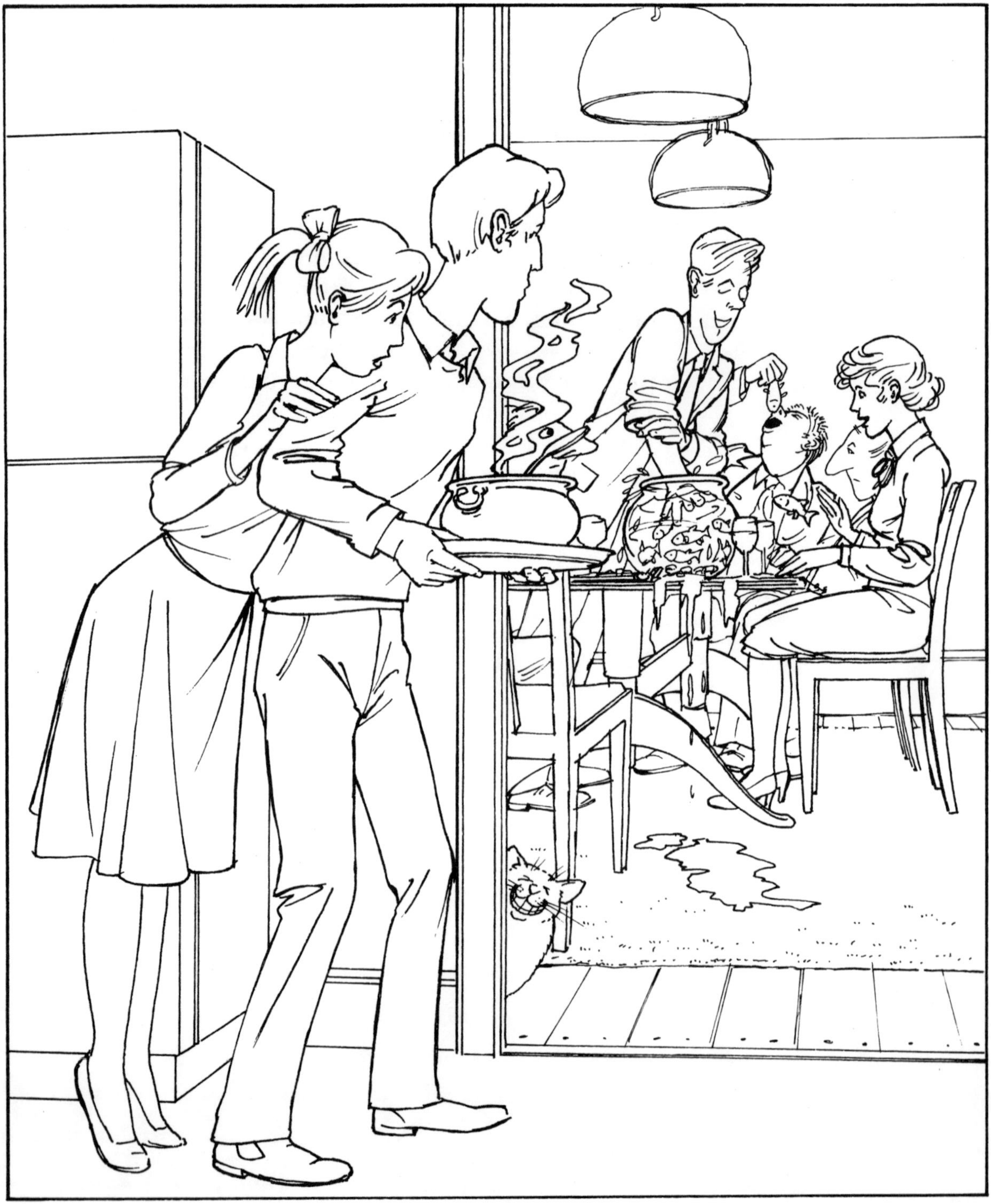

Chapter 6

Guz-Before
or
First Impressions Last

> **How you start a meal is very important – it sets the tone for the whole meal. Get this right and you've won half the battle. You don't need a huge repertoire of these but you do need to present them well. Where the Guz-in-the-Middle is a hefty one don't give them too much starter; it is not being mean, it's just giving them a chance to enjoy the pudding. (NB: this does not seem to apply to Americans, at least if their restaurants are anything to go by.)**

Soups: here are four ideas, one cold for summer, two that are hot for the rest of the year and one that can't make up its mind.

(Note: the preparation times include time for washing up as you go along, the cooking times do not include time for washing up after. The recipes are for four people unless a different number is specified in the text; of course this is also dependent on the greed of the individuals concerned.)

Cucumber Soup à la Suze

(Preparation and cooking time 30 mins)

A super summer soup (summer soup some are not – ouch!). Even those who hate cucumber have been known to like this. This is an excellent soup to serve for a meal where there is a great deal of last-minute preparation for the main course, since the soup can be made an hour or so in advance and the final touches only take a few seconds.

Ingredients

2 cucumbers
1 small onion
clove garlic
2 oz/50 gm butter
1½ pint/1 litre chicken stock
black pepper
salt
2 tablespoons cornflour
small carton (5 fl oz/150 ml) single cream

Method

Peel the onion and chop it finely. Peel and crush the garlic clove. Melt the butter in a large saucepan and add the onion and the garlic. Fry gently until the onion is soft (5 minutes). Wash and partly peel the cucumbers leaving several strips of the green skin intact (this gives the soup a good colour). Save one middle quarter of a cucumber for decoration. Chop the rest of the cucumber into sugar-lump-sized chunks. Add the cucumber to the onions and garlic in the pan and continue cooking until the cucumber chunks lose their sharp edges. Add the chicken stock, salt and pepper to taste and simmer for 5 minutes. Take the saucepan off the heat and allow the soup to cool a little.

Pour the contents of the saucepan into a blender, blend until smooth. (Unless you have an enormous blender, you will need to do this in batches, so you will need a bowl to hold the blended soup as each batch is finished.) Pour all the blended soup back into the saucepan. You can use one of those hand-held blenders for this, in which case you do everything in the saucepan.

Mix the cornflour with the cream (save half the cream for decoration). Add the cream and cornflour mix to the blended soup and simmer gently while it thickens, stirring constantly at first with a wooden spoon. Simmer for a further 10 minutes. Take the soup off the heat and let it cool down completely. This soup is served cool but not cold.

To serve: Pour the soup into individual bowls, decorate with very thin cucumber slices and a swirl of cream poured over the back of a teaspoon onto the surface of the soup. A grating of black pepper tops the whole lot off.

Carrot and Orange and Tomato Soup

(Preparation and cooking time 50 mins)

This can be done plain or with added spice; either way it is a filling, colourful and attractive way to kick off.

Ingredients

½ lb/225 gm carrots
2 large oranges
½ lb/225 gm tomatoes (skinned and seeded)
salt and pepper
Worcestershire sauce
(optionally curry powder and
½ oz/10 gm butter)
water or stock as required/preferred
cream (optional)

Method

You really will find this easier with a blender or a processor (at the very least you will need the grater). Put the carrots and tomatoes in the blender and purée. If you don't have a blender then get to work with the grater. Grate the zest of the oranges into the purée together with their juice, if necessary thinning the mixture with water or stock. Add the Worcestershire sauce. Simmer the mixture on a low heat for 40 minutes.

Alternatively, you can make this more spicy by frying a teaspoon of curry powder in ½ oz of butter and stirring it into the soup prior to simmering. If you want to make it look pretty then gently spoon a little cream on the top of the soup when it is in the serving bowls and stir gently to get a marbled effect.

French Onion Soup

(Preparation time 15 mins, cooking time 30 mins)

Many things are served under the title of French Onion Soup, but this is a good one; what is more it's easy.

Ingredients

½ lb/225 gm onions
1½ pint/1 litre stock
2 oz/50 gm butter
½ oz/10 gm flour
salt/pepper
bayleaf
French bread
cheese

Method

Cut the onions in half then slice the halves and separate the rings. Bring the stock to the boil. Sauté the onions in the butter until they are evenly browned. Mix in the flour and add the boiling stock, season to taste and put in the bayleaf. Simmer for 30 minutes and remove the bayleaf. Slice the French bread, cut a thin slice of cheese to go on top of each slice. Place the slices, cheese side uppermost, under a grill and melt the cheese until it is just starting to bubble and go brown. Serve the soup with one of these slices in each bowl.

Leek and Potato Soup (AKA Vichyssoise)

(Preparation time 20 mins, cooking time 35 mins)

The only difference between these two soups is how much you purée it and an overnight stopover in the refrigerator. Either way it is very good indeed.

Ingredients

6 large leeks
1 large potato
1 stick of celery
2 oz/50 gm butter
4 fl oz/200 ml double cream
two sprigs of fresh parsley
salt and pepper to taste
1½ pints/1 litre home-made chicken soup (essential for vichyssoise, stock cube version OK for hot)

Method

Bring the stock to the boil and then simmer until needed. Peel and slice the potato. Chop the white parts of the leeks and discard the green. Fry these slowly in butter for 5 minutes in the bottom of a small cast-iron casserole or a heavy-bottomed pan. Add the potato and stir thoroughly. After a couple of minutes pour in the simmering stock, add the parsley, celery and salt and pepper to taste. Simmer for a further 30 minutes. Remove the celery and parsley and bin them or feed them to the 'globerter-globerter' machine. Allow the mixture to cool for 10 minutes. Purée in a food processor or use a blender briefly so that it still has quite a bit of texture, adding the cream whilst processing. Return to the heat in a clean saucepan, add more seasoning if required, simmer for 2 to 3 minutes and serve.

For vichyssoise, purée more than above, until very smooth, and chill overnight.

Soup's all very well, but for those who prefer starters with more of a bite

Smoked Fish *(Preparation time 10 mins)*

An easy starter to produce; there is no cooking time, only preparation time, about ten minutes for six people.

Ingredients

As many as you like from:
smoked trout
smoked salmon
smoked mackerel
kipper (get traditional smoked ones, not the yellow dyed sort)

Allow about two to four oz (50 to 100 gm) of smoked fish per person

Method

Make a pattern on the plate using different coloured smoked fish, perhaps a small amount of fish roe (smoked cod's roe is excellent) as a centrepiece (you could call it a codpiece if you've a mind to). Some slices of avocado can be served to give a contrast of texture and taste. Serve with plain brown bread and butter.

Smoked Salmon with Dill Sauce *(Preparation time 10 mins)*

This is a really good combination of tastes. Some purists say that you should have nothing with smoked salmon other than lemon, black pepper and Champagne. We disagree.

(That means he does. – S.)

Ingredients

2 oz/50 gm smoked salmon per person (minimum)
dill sauce (buy it ready made!)

Method

Lay the salmon out in thin slices on a medium-sized plate. Serve with the sauce in a small ramekin dish for each person (then they can choose for themselves). Thin brown bread and butter should accompany this.

Melon with Parma Ham

(Preparation time 10 to 15 mins)

This is easy and refreshing. Ogen or Charentais melons have by far the best flavour for this combination.

Ingredients

1 melon per four to six people
Parma ham (2–3 slices per person)

Method

Cut the melon into longitudinal segments. Cut the ham into slices and make into small rolls.
Arrange attractively on the plate and serve with freshly ground black pepper.

Warm Chicken Liver Salad

(Preparation and cooking time 30 mins maximum)

The final stage of this starter needs to be put together quickly and served while still warm, so choose it for a meal where the second course needs no special attention at the last minute.

Ingredients (for six)

1 medium head of crisp lettuce (Frisée, Iceberg, Cos)
1 bunch watercress
1 head chicory
2 tubs chicken livers (8 oz/225 gm in all)
tablespoon plain flour
1 to 2 oz (25 to 50 gm) unsalted butter
Dijon mustard
4 tablespoons dry sherry or wine vinegar
small teaspoon caster sugar
flake sea salt
fresh French bread

Method

First prepare a salad bowl for each person; choose bowls with enough room to rummage about in for the salad leaves, dressing and the pieces of liver without scattering them all over the dining table. Wash, dry and tear the lettuce and chicory into manageable pieces; arrange them in the bowls. Wash and dry the watercress, discard the thicker, tougher stalks and divide the watercress amongst the bowls so that there is a little island of watercress in the lettuce and chicory pieces.

Mix together 4 tablespoons of dry sherry (or good wine vinegar) with 2 teaspoons of Dijon mustard with a small teaspoon of caster sugar.

You can pre-prepare up to this point and keep the salad fresh in the fridge (remember to make room for this!) until the last minute.

Last-minute stuff:
Wash, dethread and dry the chicken livers, chop roughly (not too small) and then turn them in the flour until each is lightly coated. Heat the butter in a heavy pan until it foams, add the chicken livers and fry briskly for 2–3 minutes until they are lightly browned and pale pink inside – don't overcook or they become leathery. Pour the sherry, sugar and mustard (or vinegar, sugar and mustard) mixture over the cooked livers and deglacé the pan (using a wooden spoon, stir and scrape until all the crusty bits are free and mixed with the liquid). Now spoon the livers and the sauce onto the salads, sprinkle with a little sea salt and serve immediately with fresh French bread on the side.

(Fill the frying pan with hot soapy water and leave to soak. Stack the rest of the washing-up and leave it for the moment – this starter will not wait!)

Onion Tartlets

(Preparation time 20 mins, cooking time 15 mins)

Once again, this is a starter that must be served immediately it is cooked. So it's wise to have the guests sitting down waiting hungrily, rather than milling around and getting seated while you watch your starter sink and go flabby. True, you can have a quick drink with the guests while the tartlets cook and you only have to lift them out of the tins when they're done – but you mustn't wait. Once the tartlets have 'deflated' they aren't nearly as good, so precision serving is called for.

Ingredients (for six)

8 oz/225 gm frozen puff pastry. (This will take between 30 minutes to 1 hour to defrost from the freezer.)
2 large Spanish onions sliced finely but not chopped. Cut the peeled onions in half, slice

Method

Roll out the pastry thinly and line 6 tartlet tins – these are larger than the sort of tins little jam tarts are usually made in and smaller than sponge-cake tins. I use mine for Yorkshire puddings, sage and onion stuffing servings and a multitude of other tarts and pies where an individual tart per person looks prettier than a slice from a larger tart.
Prick the pastry cases all over (especially the sides) with a fork.

them and then cut the
slices into thirds.
3 large eggs
small carton of double
cream
2–3 oz/50 to 75 gm
unsalted butter
pepper and salt

Gently fry the onion in the butter until the onions are transparent (10 minutes). Spoon the onion into the cases and season with a little salt and pepper.
Beat the eggs and the cream together and pour into the cases.
Bake in a hot oven (220°C/425°F/gas mark 7) for about 15 minutes. Serve immediately.

(I think using frozen pastry is cheating, but Suzy insisted. – D.)

Smoked Salmon Mousse

(Preparation time 15 mins)

This is about the easiest pâté/mousse that you're ever going to find.

Ingredients

½ lb/225 gm smoked salmon offcuts
large pot of cream (10 fl oz/280 ml)
lemon juice (one lemon's worth)
black pepper

Method

Throw the lot in a blender/food processor and switch it on. Don't make it too fine, it should have texture. Serve in ramekin dishes or a larger bowl from which everyone helps themselves.
Or serve it in a mouse-shaped mould and call it a mouse?

King Prawns with Dressing

(Preparation time 5 mins)

Ingredients

fresh (very) king prawns
salad dressing (see Chapter 7)

Method

Provide each person with two or three prawns (or more depending on size and appetites) and serve the dressing in a sauce boat with a spoon or small ladle.
A green salad can be provided if you wish.

Unexpected Starter *(Preparation time 5 to 10 mins, cooking time 10 mins)*

This is something you can throw together in no time flat when unexpected guests arrive for a meal you didn't know you were cooking. It is mock home-made tomato soup – sort of one better than a packet or a tin – and almost as fast.

Ingredients (for six servings)
tinned tomatoes (2 large tins or 4 small)
5 fl oz/150 ml cream (optional)
6 oz/150 gm bacon
1 large onion
salt and pepper
Worcestershire sauce
butter and 1 tablespoon flour (if you need to thicken the soup)
mixed herbs (or fresh chopped basil if you have it)
10 fl oz/300 ml stock (or vegetable stock cube and water)

Method
Finely chop the onion and the bacon and fry in the butter. Blend in the flour. Open the tins. Purée the tomatoes with the stock, add salt, pepper, herbs and Worcestershire sauce (a few drops). Mix with the bacon/onion blend, bring to the boil and simmer for about 10 minutes. Stir in the cream (if you're using it) and turn off the heat. If you are out of cream you can thicken the soup with a little flour mixed with melted butter. To make it look nice, float a teaspoon's worth of cream in and gently swirl it into a spiral pattern on the top of the soup (if you don't have any cream, just serve as is).

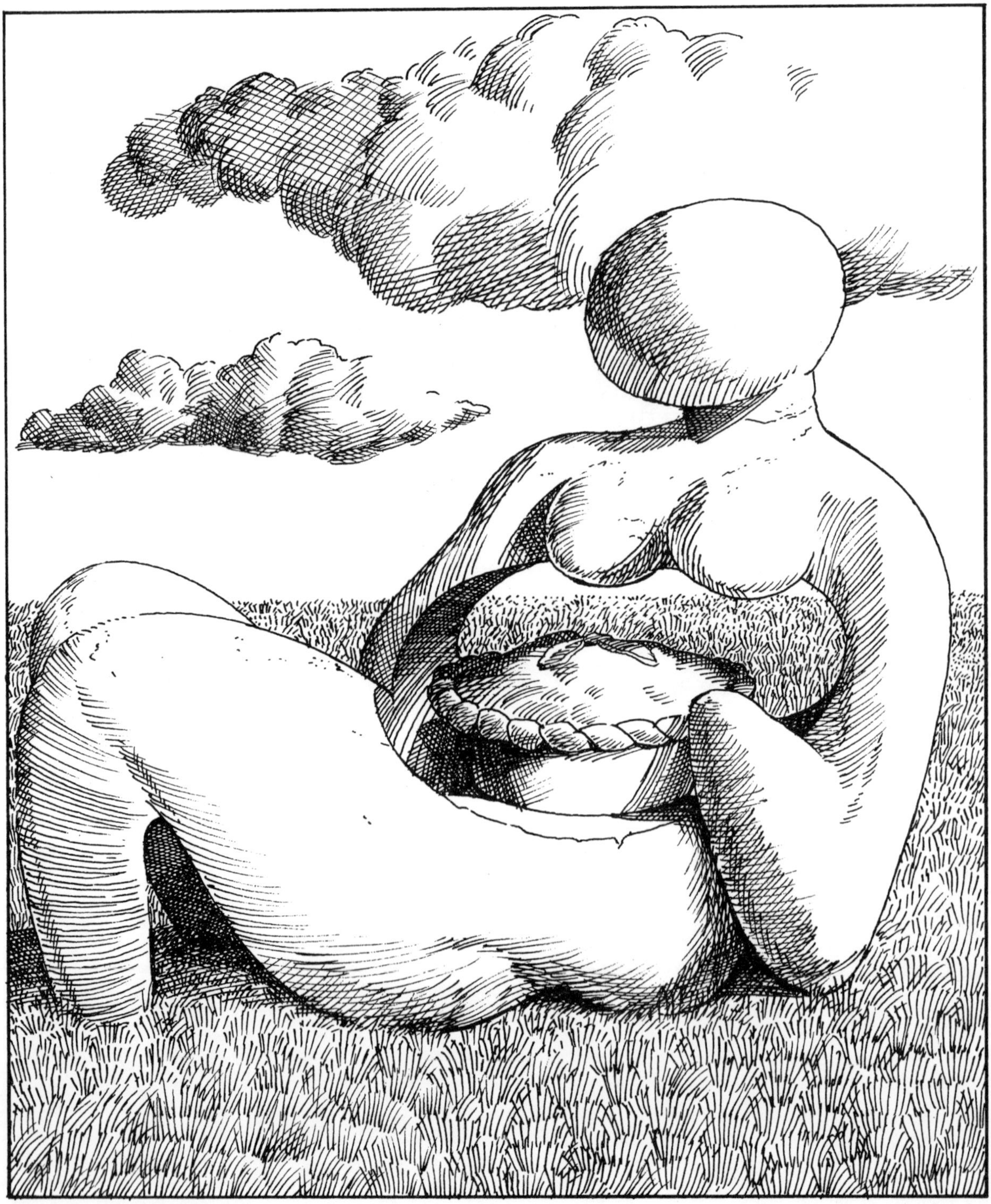

Chapter 7

Guz-in-the-Middle
or
If It Was Whale Meat They'd Only Blubber

> **Once you've got their tastebuds limbered up with your fantastic starter you are ready to conquer their hearts (through their stomachs) with the *pièce de résistance*, the main course. It doesn't matter how well you start and finish a meal, it's what 'guz-in-the-middle' that really counts.**

Note: The recipes in this chapter serve six people unless a different number is specified in the text. However, this is dependent on the greed of the individuals concerned.

Vegetables: We've put them in first because they are not the also-rans of the dinner table, but vital to the success of any meal.

Carrots, peas, new potatoes, broccoli, cabbage, Brussels sprouts. These are all best when steamed. The following table shows how long they need to be steamed. If you use a multitiered steamer, you can simply add the vegetables that need less time after the others have started cooking and they will be ready at the same time.

Steaming Times for Vegetables

Vegetable	Time Required
Carrots	15 to 20 minutes
Peas (frozen)	8 to 10 minutes
Peas (fresh)	25 minutes
New Potatoes	20 minutes
Cabbage	5 minutes
Broccoli	5 to 8 minutes
Brussels Sprouts	10 to 15 minutes

Endive/Chicory

Method

Baked chicory is a simple and unusual vegetable to serve with roasts. Remove the outer leaves and wrap the heart in aluminium foil with a knob of butter. Place in an oven at 175°C/350°F/gas mark 4 and bake for 30 minutes. They should then be unwrapped and served.

Salads: These can be either very simple or very complicated. The golden rule for a good salad, however, is always the same – use fresh, high quality ingredients and make it as near to serving time as you can. Above all else, avoid limp lettuce salads.

Salad Dressing (AKA French Dressing)

The perfect tool for making salad dressing is one of those translucent screw-top bottles that fresh orange juice comes in.

Ingredients

6 tablespoons good olive oil
½ teaspoon Dijon mustard
2 tablespoons wine vinegar
¼ teaspoon salt
¼ teaspoon fresh black pepper
1 teaspoon sugar

Method

Pour all the ingredients into the bottle, screw on the top and shake the bottle like fury. Pour into suitable jug for serving. Try varying the proportions of the ingredients to tune the salad to your own taste.

Tomato Salad   Couldn't be simpler. Take one medium-sized tomato per person and slice it up. Place in a bowl or on a serving dish and pour on some salad dressing.

Potato Salad

Ingredients

2 lb/900 gm new potatoes, scrubbed but not peeled
1 bunch spring onions chopped
3 oz/75 gm butter
French dressing (see above)

Method

While the potatoes are hot, mix in the butter and chopped spring onions and pour on the dressing. Serve warm.

Simple Green Salad

Ingredients

lettuce
cucumber
chicory
radishes

About 2 to 4 oz/50 to 100 gm per person in total

Method

Use the freshest ingredients you can get. Wash them and chop them into 'forkable' pieces, mix up in a suitable bowl with some French dressing, serve chilled from the refrigerator.

Now to the food proper . . .
Roast Pheasant   *(Preparation time 10 mins, cooking time 45 mins)*

These are in season from October to January, and although frozen ones are available all year round, we think this is when you should eat them. One bird should just about serve four people, so if you have a dinner party for six, use two and give the cats a treat with the leftovers. Don't be misled by the macho values of some game enthusiasts – the meat should not be hung until it is dropping to pieces and reeks of ammonia. Pheasants should be fresh, so make sure yours is.

Ingredients

1 drawn, fresh (definitely unhung) pheasant per 4 folk
red wine (about ⅓/½ a bottle)
4 oz/110 gm butter
streaky bacon (4 rashers)
salt and black pepper
herbes de Provence
5 fl oz/150 ml stock

Method

Season the bird with salt, pepper, and herbs. Preheat the oven to 200°C/400°F/gas mark 6. Fry the seasoned bird in the butter (in a frying pan, of course) until it is a nice golden brown all over. Transfer to a roasting tin with the bird, right breast down, basted with butter from the pan. Cook for 15 minutes. Take it out of oven, baste, return it to oven with the other breast down for a further 15 minutes. Remove from the oven, put the bird on its back, cover with the bacon, rebaste and add the wine. Return it to the oven for a further 10 to 15 minutes, or until it is cooked. Test it by prodding a leg (the bird's, not yours!). When it is done, remove it from the oven and allow it to rest while you make the gravy. Pour any juices from inside the bird into the roasting tin and transfer it to the hob. Heat it up until it has bubbled for a couple of minutes, then add the stock and stir. Add salt and pepper to taste. Serve with small roast potatoes and petits pois or mangetout. A good Burgundy or a Châteauneuf-du-Pape will go well with this meal.

Steak and Kidney Pie

(Preparation time 40 mins, cooking time 2 hours)

Snake and pigmy is wonderful for cold, damp winter evenings when your guests come in dripping wet and chilled to the marrow because they had to walk ten miles across the heathlands after their car broke down. Even we townies understand that sort of feeling; at least we do if the central heating gets a fit of the vapours. This recipe does take a bit of time to prepare and cook, but it is worth it every time.

Ingredients

2 lb/900gm braising steak
½ lb/225 gm ox kidney
2 onions
2 carrots
1 clove garlic
1 oz/25 gm flour (seasoned with salt, pepper and herbs)
½ pint/300 ml stock

Pastry (shortcrust)
8 oz/225 gm flour (sifted)
pinch of salt
4 oz/110 gm butter (cold)
iced water

Glaze:
1 egg yolk beaten with some milk

(David insists on making things difficult. I use frozen pastry. – S.)

Method

Pastry: Sift flour and salt into a basin. Cut the butter into small pieces. Use the blade of a knife to mix the butter with the flour/salt mixture, then use fingertips to rub it into the flour until it resembles sugar. Add a little iced water, mixing with a knife until you have dough which holds together. Wrap this in Clingfilm (or put it in a resealable plastic bag) and chill in the refrigerator for 20 minutes. Roll out until the pastry is ⅓ inch thick.

Filling: Thinly slice the carrots and onions. Cut the meat into one-inch chunks and toss in the seasoned flour. Put layers of meat, onions and carrots into a heavy, metal casserole or saucepan with lid and top up with the stock. Bring to the boil and simmer. Add salt and pepper to taste.

After the filling has been simmered for an hour and a half, put it into the pie dish and cover with the pastry and trim. Use offcuts to make any decorations you need for the top of the pie (e.g. leaf shapes). Glaze with the egg yolk mixture. Transfer to a preheated oven (200°C/400°F/gas mark 6) and bake for 30 minutes or until the pastry is golden brown.

Target Chicken

(Preparation time 20 mins, cooking time 20 to 30 mins)

This is named after the appearance of the finished product – a set of white, pink and green targets laid out along a diameter of the plate. It is a very impressive and rich looking meal which doesn't actually take all that long to do. What's more it is fairly healthy too.

Ingredients	Method
chicken supremes (skinned, chicken breasts), one per person smoked salmon (offcuts will do), 2 oz/50 gm per person asparagus (3 sticks per person minimum) lemon sauce (juice of ½ lemon per person, mixed 50/50 with chicken stock, simmered for 5 minutes)	Preheat the oven to 190°C/375°F/gas mark 5. Steam the asparagus for about 10 minutes and put to one side. Cut the bone off the end of the supremes and make a lengthwise pouch with a sharp knife. Line this with smoked salmon bits. Cut a piece of asparagus to length and put it inside the salmon-lined pouch. Tie up the package with some string and place it on a baking tray. Cook in the oven for 20–30 minutes until cooked – the time will depend on the size of the pieces. While it's cooking, make the lemon sauce.

When it has cooked, slice the supremes crosswise. You should now have a set of white, pink and green targets. Serve with asparagus, mangetout, lemon sauce and boiled new potatoes. |

Headline Trout

(Preparation time 10 mins, cooking time 30 mins)

So called because traditionally you use newspaper for this recipe. If you don't like the thought of bad news contaminating your dinner, then use brown paper instead.

Ingredients	Method
1 trout (gutted, heads optional) per person enough paper to wrap up the fish	This couldn't be simpler. Preheat the oven to 190°C/380°F/gas mark 5. Rinse the trout under the tap and dry off with kitchen paper. Soak the news-/brown paper in water and wrap the fish in it – brown paper is best though newspaper has merit.
Place them on a baking tray in the oven and cook for 30 minutes, or until all the paper is dry. When you take them out of the oven unwrap them and the skin should come off with the paper.

Chicken Transit (after Coq au Vin)

(Preparation time 30 mins, cooking time 2 hours)

Cockerels being hard to come by these days, most people use a chicken. It is also a meal more sinned against than sinning, judging by the variety of products that get served up under the banner 'Coq au Vin'. This is our version and jolly good it is too.

Ingredients

medium (4 people) to large (just about 6 people) chicken
a bottle of reasonable St Emilion, or good, if you feel extravagant
4 large onions
2 cloves garlic
8 oz/225 gm bacon
4 oz/125 gm butter
1 tablespoon flour
½ glass cooking brandy
1 pint/600 ml stock
4 oz/125 gm button mushrooms

Method

The most important thing with this recipe is to make sure that it is cooked long enough. This is best cooked in a cast-iron enamelled casserole. Melt half the butter in the bottom of the casserole. Cut the bacon into one-inch squares and fry it with the chicken and the onions until they are all browned. Crush the garlic and add it to the fat. Flame with a little brandy. Add the wine, the herbs, salt, pepper and the stock. Bring slowly to the boil and simmer for 1½ to 2 hours – the chicken should not actually fall off the bone but it should be loose. If you have actually got hold of a cockerel or you're cooking an old hen, then it will be nearer to 3 hours. Now remove the chicken from the pan and keep warm in a low oven. Put the mushrooms into the sauce and boil for 5 to 10 minutes. Thicken the sauce with melted butter mixed with some plain flour if necessary.

Suzy's Carbonnade of Beef

(Preparation time 40 minutes, cooking time 2 hours)

This is based on a traditional recipe, but has evolved over the years. It may not be completely authentic but it tastes wonderful. In autumn have it with hot vegetables, in spring with a green side salad and some new potatoes, in winter with baked potatoes.

Ingredients

2 cans Guinness
2 large onions chopped
¼ lb Gruyère cheese grated
1 long stick French bread
Dijon mustard
2 oz/50 gm plain flour
2 lb/900 gm stewing steak cut into 2-inch/5-cm chunks
2 tablespoons olive oil
3 oz/75 gm butter
2 tablespoons good wine vinegar
1 tablespoon brown sugar
salt, pepper, nutmeg, allspice, bay leaf (to taste)
2 cloves garlic (crushed)
Worcestershire sauce
4 large field mushrooms or ½ lb button mushrooms optional
1 lb/450 gm small carrots
8 oz/225 gm frozen petits pois

Method

Toss the meat in the flour. Heat half the butter and olive oil in a heavy pan and fry the meat, a few pieces at a time, until browned. Remove each batch of meat as it is cooked and keep warm. Pour any juices remaining in the pan over the cooked meat. In a separate casserole (large enough to take the finished carbonnade), fry the onions in the remaining butter and oil until browned. Stir constantly. Add the crushed garlic and the sugar and cook for 2 more minutes. Now pour the Guinness into the casserole and add the meat, a few shakes of Worcestershire sauce, spices and seasonings and bay leaf and bring to a brisk simmer. Put into a medium oven (150°C/300°F/gas mark 2) and cook slowly for 2 hours. (If you like, you can add sliced carrots at this point to make the meal heartier.) Now do the washing-up!

After 2 hours, add the roughly chopped mushroom and petits pois if you like them and cook for another half an hour. All this can be done the day before and, in fact, the casserole gets tastier if you do this.

On the day, three-quarters of an hour before you need to serve, slice the baguette into 1 inch slices, spread each with Dijon mustard and arrange on top of the 'stew'. Sprinkle liberally with Gruyère cheese and put into a medium hot oven (170°C/325°F/gas mark 3). When the cheese is melted and the stew heated through, it's ready to serve.

For those of you who like to cook with as little fat as possible, it is OK simply to put the floured meat, chopped onions, garlic, flavourings, Guinness and optional carrots into the casserole all at once and bring to the boil, stirring constantly; then cook in the oven as before.

Steak au Poivre *(Preparation time 5 mins, cooking time 5 to 20 mins)*

Steaks are tricky things to do for dinner parties. They have to be cooked to order. But with one of you to entertain the guests, the other lucky person can be ze master chef, particularly useful if that person doesn't feel like making small talk with the guests. Make sure that you get the best steak available as success depends on it.

Ingredients (for 4 people)

4 to 6 oz fillet steak (1 inch thick) per person
green peppercorns
2 oz/50 gm butter
Dijon mustard
red wine (one glass)
2 fl oz/50 ml cream

Method

Crush the peppercorns in a pestle and mortar. Melt the butter in a frying pan and get it nice and hot then add the peppercorns. Cook the steaks in this, turning every minute or so to ensure even cooking. You will need to cook them to order: 1 minute each side gives very rare, suitable for a Frenchman, 5 minutes each side is medium, 10 minutes gives very well done. You will probably have to experiment at home before you are really able to cook to order – practice will make perfect. When all the steaks are ready (you can keep them warm in a *very* low oven for a few minutes while the well done one catches up with the rare), turn down the heat, mix in the wine and reduce for a few minutes. Then, just before you are ready to serve, mix in the cream and spoon the sauce over the steaks. Accompany the meat with new potatoes and a green salad.

Chicken Curry with Saffron Rice *(Preparation time 20 mins, cooking time 1 hour minimum)*

This is by no means an authentic recipe. It uses curry powder and the Indians do not. They don't even mix their own. They use individual, whole spices in different combinations for different recipes. However, it does provide a wonderful spicy meal which has been accepted by both curry lovers and haters alike. It is a very anglicised meal. If you want to experiment, adding more ginger will give it more bite and a dry heat.

Adding more cumin and turmeric will round out the aromatic flavours. Adding yoghurt will make it richer and smoother (do this near the end of the cooking rather than at the beginning). But be careful, vary only one spice at a time and don't change the quantities by too much either. Alternatively, just use the proprietary curry powder as it comes.

Ingredients (serves 4 to 6 depending on appetite)

medium strength curry powder 3 teaspoons
ginger (optional) up to 1 teaspoon
cumin (optional) up to 1 teaspoon
turmeric (optional) up to 1 teaspoon
2 cloves garlic
1 large onion, finely chopped
4 oz/110 gm mushrooms
1 pint chicken stock
4 chicken supremes cut into ½-inch cubes
tinned tomatoes, (1 large tin)
Worcestershire sauce, (a dash)
2 oz/50 gm rice per person (long grain or Basmati – read the packet for any special instructions)

Method

Bring the stock to the boil and simmer. Fry the onion in the oil until transparent, add crushed garlic and stir for about 30 seconds. Put the chicken into the pan and seal on all sides. Add the spices and stir in well until all the chicken is coated. Add the tinned tomatoes and break them up with a wooden spoon; mix in the fresh herbs and the bay leaf. Pour in the stock and simmer for 30 minutes. Turn off the heat and rest for 30 minutes (can be longer) to let the flavours mingle. Slice the mushrooms and add to the mixture. Return to the heat and simmer for a further 30 minutes; add the yoghurt if desired. This curry will benefit from being left to cool for a few hours, reheating to serve. It will also freeze and can then be microwaved for instant meals.

Saffron rice has a light yellow colour and a golden, honeyed taste. It is very easy to make. Cover the rice with 2½ times its own volume of water, add some strands of saffron and bring to the boil from cold until cooked (the water will have been absorbed). Rinse if necessary, depending on the rice, and serve.

Noodles Quattro Formaggio

(Actually, like all recipes that I learnt 'authentically' it has been gradually 'unauthenticated' over the years, so this is the general version. – S.)

(Preparation time 40 mins, cooking time 40 mins)

This will do for vegetarians if you leave out the bacon. Suzy learnt to cook this in Venice, so this is an authentic recipe. (We must be slipping up somewhere.)

Ingredients (for 6)

2 lb/900 gm green ribbon noodles (tagliatelli)
2 oz/50 gm each: Parmesan (freshly grated), Dolcelatte (or any mild blue cheese), Gruyère (or any hard but meltable cheese), and Cheddar
1 clove garlic, crushed
1 large onion, finely chopped
1 large tin peeled tomatoes
fresh basil, herbes de Provence or mixed herbs
½ lb thin cut streaky bacon, chopped
2 oz/50 gm plain flour
2 oz/50 gm unsalted butter
1 pint milk
olive oil
seasoning

Method

Fry the onion and garlic in the olive oil until transparent. Add the tinned tomatoes, herbs and seasoning and simmer gently for 10 minutes.
Fry the bacon in a little olive oil until cooked and slightly crisp.
Put the butter and flour into a nonstick saucepan. Cook, stirring constantly until they don't smell of flour but haven't changed colour. Remove from the heat, pour all the milk into the pan and stir with a wire whisk until blended. Return to a low heat and stir with a wooden spoon until it thickens. Add the cheese, grated or cut into small pieces and continue stirring until you have a velvety sauce. Keep warm.
Boil the tagliatelli in plenty of water with a teaspoon of olive oil to prevent sticking, until *al dente*; drain and keep warm. Now, in a casserole, compile the dish.
A layer of cheese sauce, a third of the tagliatelli, a layer of tomato sauce, a sprinkle of bacon, repeat this twice ending with a topping of the cheese sauce.
Put into a medium oven (150°C/300°F/gas mark 2) and cook through for 30 minutes.
Serve with French bread and a green salad.

Unexpected Main Course

(Preparation time 10 mins, cooking time 15 mins)

As with the **Unexpected Starter** this is a recipe for providing you with a meal for the unexpected guests. You should have all the necessary bits and pieces in the cupboards/refrigerator. From doorbell to plate in under 30 minutes, the Ferrari of the dinner table. Pasta is faster, so it's **Tagliatelli Carbonara**, though you can use any other type of pasta if you wish.

Ingredients (for 4 people)

1 lb/450 gm tagliatelli
1 clove garlic
10 fl oz/300 ml cream
3 eggs
6 oz/175 gm bacon (streaky with rind removed)
2 tablespoons olive oil
salt and black pepper

Method

The best pans for cooking this are a cast-iron casserole for the frying and a stockpot for boiling the pasta. In a mixing bowl, whisk the eggs and cream together and put aside, add salt and pepper to taste. Boil the water and cook the pasta in it for 10 minutes, or until *al dente*. Whilst that is happening, cut the bacon into small pieces and fry in the hot oil in the casserole with crushed garlic and diced onions. After it is cooked, turn off the heat and pour off the excess oil. When the pasta is cooked, pour off the water and transfer to the casserole and mix it up with the bacon and onions. Now pour the cream/egg mixture over the top and leave for about 2 minutes. The residual heat in the casserole and the pasta will cook the sauce. Serve immediately with Parmesan cheese and black pepper to taste. You may accompany this with a green salad.

> "To make a good salad is to be a brilliant diplomatist – the problem is exactly the same in both cases. To know exactly how much oil one must put with one's vinegar."
> *Oscar Wilde*

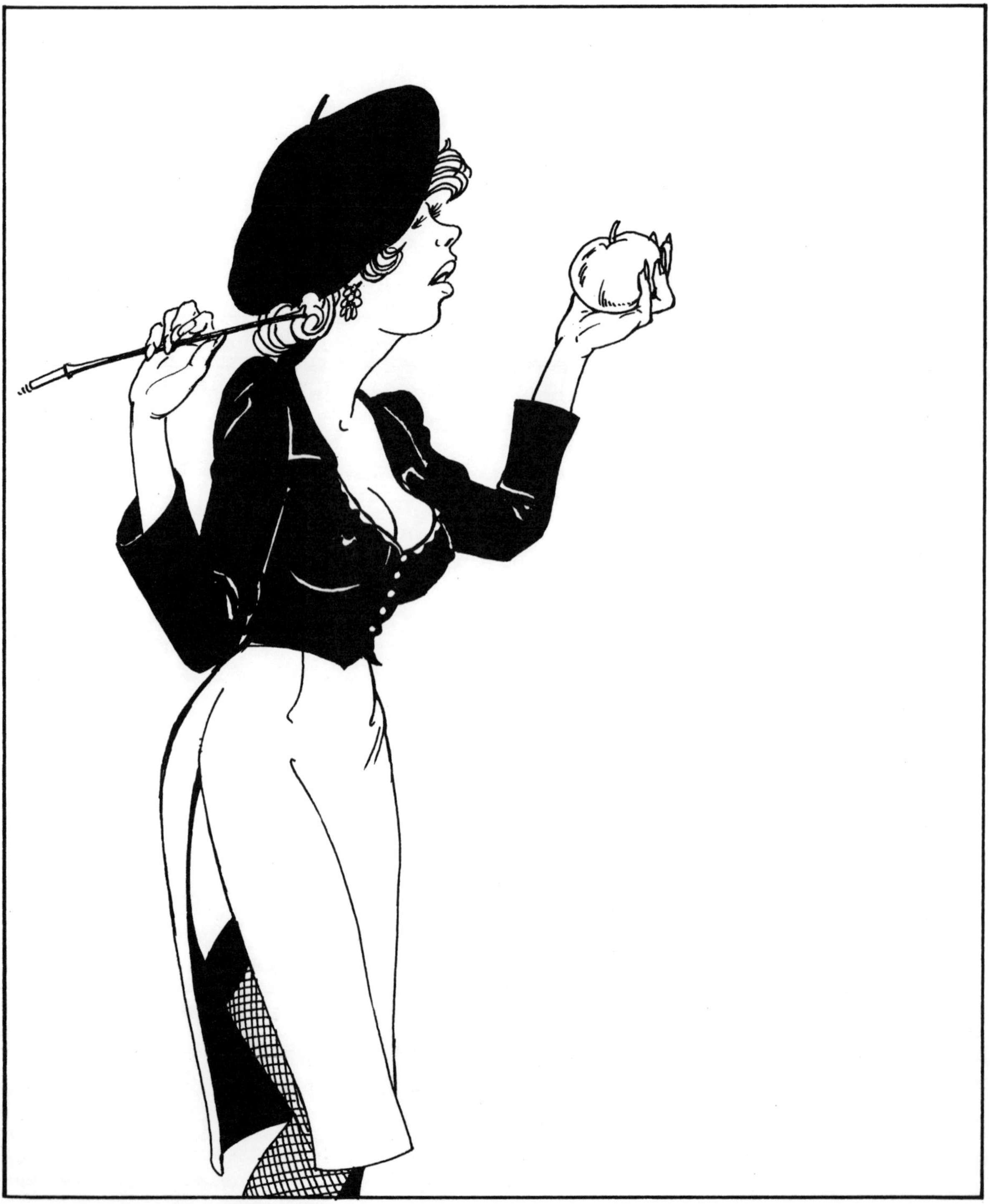

Chapter 8

Guz-After
or
The Sweet Get Just Desserts

> **By the time people have got this far, they have probably had an elegant sufficiency of food. So don't overdo the quantities, they can always be offered more. It is often a good idea to have a gap between the main course and the Guz-After anyway, even if it's only for an intercourse cigarette for the smokers amongst you.**

Note: The recipes in this chapter serve six people unless a different number is specified in the text. However, this is dependent on the greed of the individuals concerned.

Fruit Salad *(Preparation time 15 to 30 mins, chilling time 1 hour)*

This slightly alcoholic offering is perfect for summer evenings on the terrace (fighting off the mosquitoes). Put a whole bunch more booze in it and you can call it punch.

Ingredients
1 lb/450 gm strawberries
2 kiwi fruit
2 bananas
2 apples

Method
Using a little heat slowly dissolve the sugar in the water, allow it to cool and add the wine. Stir well. Destalk/peel/core, slice and chop the fruit into roughly 1 cm thick chunks. Place them in a salad bowl and cover with the orange juice and sugar/wine mixture.

4 fl oz/100 ml fresh orange juice
7 fl oz/200 ml fruity white wine (preferably Alsace)
4 oz/110 gm sugar
4 fl oz/100 ml water

Chill in the refrigerator for at least 1 hour before serving.

French Apple Tart *(Preparation time 20 to 30 mins, cooking time 40 mins)*

This is best served cold (though you can eat it hot). It is perfect at all times of the year. The secret of a good apple tart is the pastry; you must think kind, loving thoughts while you make it. If you have the time, make it by hand, not in a food processor; it is very good exercise for you.

Ingredients

Pastry
8 oz/225 gm plain flour, sifted with a pinch of salt
½ oz/10 gm icing sugar
5 oz/150 gm cold butter
1 egg yolk
fresh lemon juice
iced water

Glaze
1 egg yolk beaten with a little milk

Filling
4 medium to large dessert apples, e.g. Granny Smiths
1 oz/25 gm caster sugar
1 oz/25 gm butter

Method

Pastry
Preheat the oven to 200°C/400°F/gas mark 6. Mix the flour, sugar and salt together and cut the butter into very small (¼ inch/1 cm) cubes. Rub the butter into the mixture using your fingertips until it forms small flakes. Add the egg yolk and a little of the iced water and mix the dough with a knife blade; add additional water to achieve the desired consistency. Form the dough into a ball and wrap in Clingfilm (or a resealable plastic bag) and chill for 20 minutes. Roll out the pastry so that it is large enough to line the baking tin. Put it into the baking tin and trim off any excess with a knife, cover with aluminium foil and bake blind in the oven for 10 minutes. Remove the foil and glaze the pastry. Cook for a further 10 minutes and allow to cool.

Filling
Core and peel the apples and halve them. Cut each half into thin slices. Overlap these in rows across the width of the baking tin. Sprinkle the rows with caster sugar

gelatine
water
juice of 1 lemon

and dot with butter. Bake for 40 minutes at 200°C/400°F/gas mark 6, then remove from oven. Make the gelatine with water according to the manufacturer's directions. To improve the flavour replace some of the water with the juice of half a lemon. Brush the apples with the lemon gelatine and allow to cool. Serve at room temperature with double cream.

Tiramisu

(Preparation time 30 mins, chilling time 30 mins or longer)

This is the passion of a beautiful, and surprisingly slim, Italian friend of ours. It takes a bit of time to make, but it tastes magnificent. This is a truly decadent dessert.

Ingredients (6 ordinary servings or 4 huge ones)
4 egg yolks
4 egg whites
4 oz/110 gm icing sugar
8 oz/250 gm Mascarpone cheese
6 sponge fingers
fresh coffee
dark rum or Marsala wine
cocoa powder
chocolate shells (6)

Method
Whisk the egg yolks with 2 oz/50 gm of icing sugar until it forms a smooth paste. Stir in the Mascarpone and beat gently, taking care not to make the mixture separate. Whisk the egg whites, adding the remaining 2 oz/50 gm of sugar a bit at a time until you have a stiff, meringue-like texture. Stir this into the mixture. Make the coffee (decaffeinated if you prefer), allow it to cool and add the rum (amount to taste). Cut the fingers in half across their length and dip in the coffee/rum mixture. Put two of the dipped, half-fingers into each chocolate shell and cover with the Mascarpone/egg mixture. If the shells are very deep you may be able to have a second layer of sponge fingers and Mascarpone. Chill for at least half an hour, then keep refrigerated until you wish to serve them (will keep overnight, but not much longer). To serve, dust the desserts with cocoa powder. Goes very well with a glass of Marsala pudding wine.

Bakewell Tart

(Preparation time 15 to 20 mins, cooking time 40 to 50 mins)

Coming from Derbyshire, David insisted that we have this one. His mother's 'Bakey Tart' is justly famed and this is her recipe (more or less).

Ingredients

Pastry
6 oz/175 gm plain flour
pinch of salt
4 oz/110 gm butter
1 oz/25 gm caster sugar
1 egg yolk
2 tablespoons iced water
a little lemon juice (optional)

Filling
raspberry or strawberry jam
1 oz/25 gm butter
2 oz/50 gm caster sugar
1 egg
2 oz/50 gm ground almonds
flaked almonds
½ lemon (grated rind and juice)
2 oz/50 gm breadcrumbs (that's two slices' worth)

Method

Make the pastry dough first, then whilst it is chilling in the refrigerator make the filling.

Pastry
Sift the flour and the salt together. Cut the butter up into small pieces (about ¼ inch/½ cm square) and rub into the flour until it looks like breadcrumbs. Mix the egg yolk with the water and blend with the flour/butter mixture. Knead into a dough and put into the refrigerator to chill wrapped in Clingfilm/greaseproof paper. Roll out on a lightly floured surface when ready.

Filling
Cream the butter and sugar in a basin until soft and smooth. Add the lemon rind and juice and beat until light. Beat the egg and add a little at a time, still beating the mixture. Stir in the ground almonds and the breadcrumbs. When you've rolled out the pastry use it to line a 7 inch flan dish. Spread the jam across the inside of the pastry. Then cover it with the filling and spread almond flakes over the top. Place in the oven and cook for 40 to 50 minutes or until done. The finished product can be served hot or cold, though we prefer it cold with cream.

Summer Fruit Fool

(Preparation and cooking time 40 mins, chilling time 1 hour)

Absolutely perfect for dealing with bumper crops of raspberries, blackberries and other soft fruits. The whisky is optional, but it helps. You can freeze these if you want to have a stock of them for winter treats. If you make too much of the fruit purée, just use it as the basis for sorbet (*see recipe following*).

Ingredients (for 6)
1 lb/450 gm of mixed summer fruits (blackberries/ raspberries/ blackcurrants and so on)
6 oz/175 gm caster sugar
¾ pint/400 ml whipping cream
malt whisky (optional)
¼ pint/150 ml water

Method
Beat the cream until it is thick. Wash, destalk and prepare the fruit. Mix the sugar with the water and bring to the boil. Simmer until the sugar has all dissolved. Add the fruit and bring back to the simmer for about 15 minutes. Allow to cool and purée with a hand-held blender. Put aside about 1 fl oz/25 ml of the purée and pour the remainder into a basin and mix the cream in. Do not do this too thoroughly – you want to have some variation in the colour. Pour the fruit fool into individual serving dishes and swirl in a teaspoon of the reserved purée to give a spiral effect on the surface. Chill until ready to serve. (This can be speeded up by judicious use of the freezing compartment.)

Sorbet

(*Preparation and cooking time 40 mins, freezing time 1 to 2 hours*)

This is another way of using up summer fruits, and we like to have a few in stock. It is based on the **Summer Fruit Fool** recipe and it is a good idea to do them both at the same time.

Ingredients
2 beaten egg whites
summer fruits

Method
As for the fruit fool, destalk and wash the fruit. Pour the sugar into the water and bring to the boil; simmer until dissolved. Add the fruit and cook for a further 15 minutes. Allow to cool a little and purée in a liquidiser or with a blender. Add whisky to taste. Pour into a suitable container and freeze for about 2 hours or until nearly solid. Transfer this to the blender again and process with the egg whites to a slushy purée. Freeze again for about 1 more hour, or until set. Take out of freezer about 10 minutes before you want to serve it. Scoop it out and serve it in Martini glasses.

Trifle (*Preparation time 45 mins*)

This is the real stuff – proper sherry trifle, not that nonsense they give you in restaurants. This is my maternal grandfather's recipe (he was a pastry chef).

Ingredients

Custard
8 fl oz/300 ml double cream
3 egg yolks
1 oz/25 gm caster sugar

Filling
1 packet ratafia biscuits
1 packet Victoria Sponge/6 trifle sponge cakes
3–4 fl oz/75–100 ml dry/medium sherry
7 fl oz/280 ml double cream (for the topping)
raspberry jam (best quality; better still home-made)

Method

Make the custard as described under **Real Custard** (Chapter 11), except using the ingredients as given here. Allow it to cool a little – while you make the trifle is long enough. Take the trifle sponges (buy them, don't make them) and cut them into slices about 1 inch by ½ inch by 3 inch. Cover them generously with the jam and use them to line the trifle dish. Scatter the ratafia biscuits (reserving 9 of them) into the dish. Use 2 or 3 glasses of sherry and sprinkle over the sponges, leave for 1 or 2 minutes to let it soak in. Pour the custard over the sponges and ratafias and place in the refrigerator until set. Whip the double cream until it is slightly peaky (or at least not very well?). Remove the trifle from the refrigerator and spread the cream on the top of the custard. Decorate with the 9 ratafia biscuits. Return to the refrigerator until an hour before serving. Trifle benefits from being made the night before – the tastes get a chance to mingle.

Crème Brûlée (*Preparation time – hours, cooking time – minutes*)

There is something marvellous about smashing in the top of one of these with the back of your spoon. Takes you right back to the nursery. The important thing is to make sure that the tops are really crisp and glassy. Make sure the serving dishes can stand the heat.

Ingredients

¾ pint/450 ml double cream
vanilla pod or vanilla essence
6 eggs
3 oz/75 gm caster sugar

Method

This takes a long time so you may wish to cook it the day/morning before.

Preheat oven to 150°C/300°F/gas mark 2. Beat the eggs in a basin with 1 oz caster sugar until smooth. Heat the cream slowly until it is about to boil, with the vanilla pod (or just add a few drops of essence) then remove the pod. Remove from heat. Pour the hot cream into the eggs, whisking all the time. Put the basin with the mixture over a pan of simmering water and stir constantly until it is thick enough to coat the back of the spoon. Pour the mixture into ramekin dishes (of a fireproof nature) and place them in the oven for 5 minutes or longer until a skin forms. Remove from the oven and leave to cool.

Set the grill to 'very fierce indeed'. Spread about ¹⁄₁₆ inch (2 to 3 mm) of caster sugar over the surface of each dish. Now place the ramekin dishes under the grill, moving them around to ensure even cooking (don't burn yourself). When the topping has melted and browned (this doesn't take very long) remove from heat, allow to cool, then chill for several hours.

Note: We have been told that it is possible to use a blowtorch to finish off this dessert. However, for some obscure reason our kitchen is not so equipped, and it's a long way to the garage. We haven't tried this, but bear it in mind for picnics.

Treacle Tart *(Preparation time 30 mins, cooking time 30 mins)*

Another thank you to David's mother and a treat for the taste buds. It is very good both hot and cold. Its tang will set you up nicely for a rich round cheese afterwards (Stilton is perfect). However, it does not go well with wine.

Ingredients

Pastry
8 oz/225 gm plain flour
pinch of salt
4 oz/110 gm butter
iced water to mix

Filling
8 fl oz/200 ml golden syrup
8 tablespoons of fresh breadcrumbs
grated rind and juice of a lemon
8 inch (20 cm) flan dish

Method

Mix the flour and salt in a bowl. Cut the butter into ½- inch (1.5 cm) cubes. Rub this into the flour using your fingertips until it has the consistency of breadcrumbs. Mix in the cold water with a knife until the dough is no longer crumbly but is not too sticky. Form into a ball and wrap in Clingfilm or a resealable plastic bag and chill in the refrigerator for half an hour before rolling out. Heat the oven to 190°C/375°F/gas mark 5. Mix the crumbs, syrup, lemon rind and juice with a fork. Pour it into the pastry case. If you wish you can cut some thin strips of pastry and use them for a decorative lattice laid on top of the mixture. Bake in the oven for 30 minutes. Serve hot with custard.

Cheese

This is a subject in its own right. Here is the minimalist approach. First of all you can serve cheese last of all, or, as the French do, you can serve it before the dessert. It's entirely up to you. You can even serve it instead of dessert. See Chapter 2 on buying cheese.

Unexpected Pudding (*Preparation time 10 mins, cooking time 10 mins*)

Yet another recipe for coping with those wretched unexpected guests. This is for a soufflé omelette.

Ingredients (per person)

2 eggs, separated
1 tablespoon cold water
butter
1 teaspoon caster sugar
1 tablespoon jam or honey

Method

Beat the egg yolks with the sugar and cold water until smooth. Whisk the whites until they are stiff and form peaks. Fold the egg yolk mixture gently into the whites. Heat the butter in an omelette or small frying pan until it is starting to brown, then reduce the heat slightly and pour in the mixture. Do not stir. Continue to cook until the omelettes start to puff up and the surface is bubbly. Spread the jam or honey over the top of the omelette and fold it in half. Serve straight away with cream if desired.

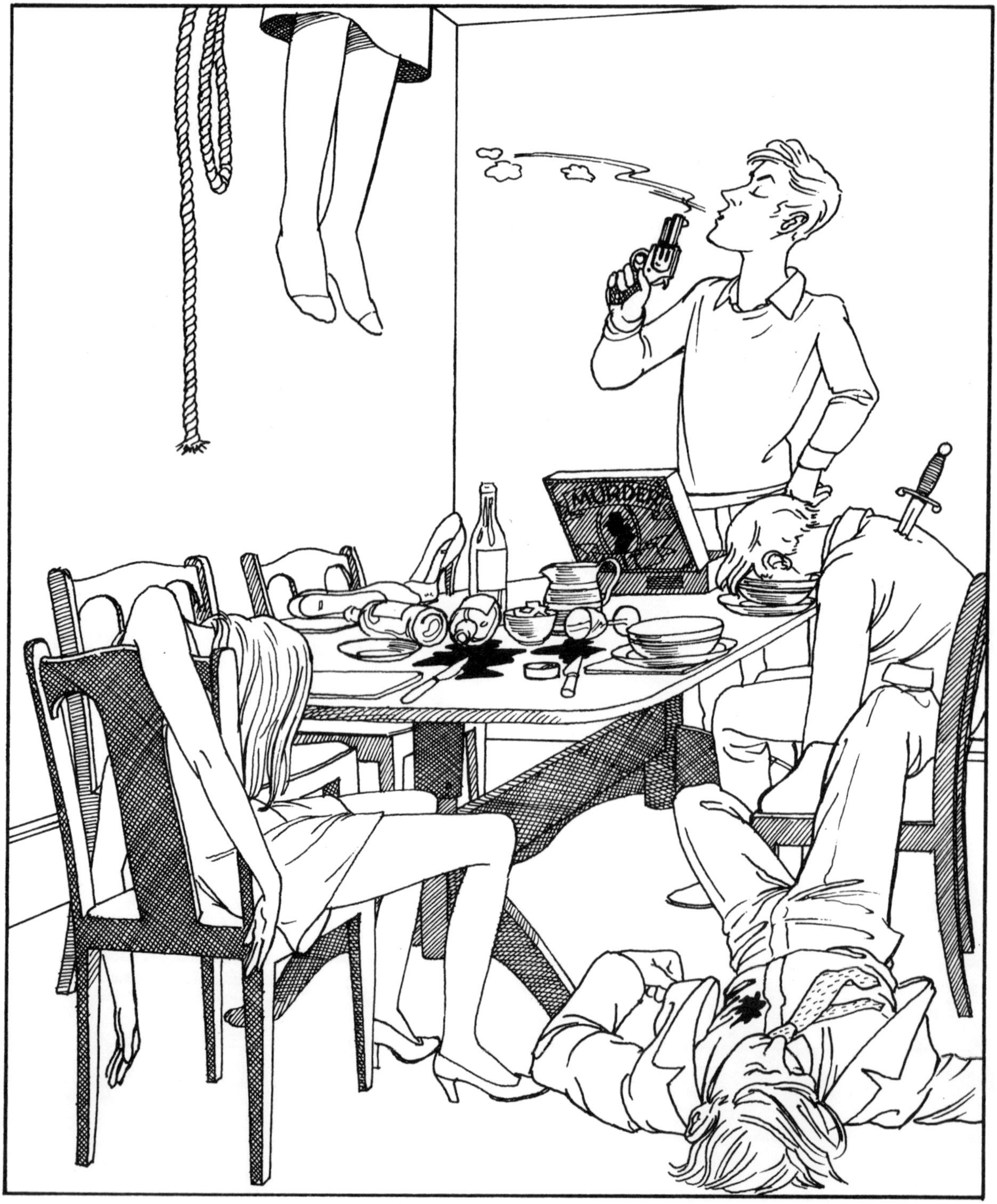
MURDER

Chapter 9

Dinner Party Games
or
Next Time It's the Holiday Snaps

> **Many people like to play games at dinner parties (footsie, spot the adulterer, carve your initials in the Georgian table and so on). We've found some alternative games to keep guests occupied when conversation flags or just for the fun of it. Hopefully you won't have to resort to too many of these.**

Alphabet This is really just a variation on Lists, but it has the advantage that you don't need pencil and paper. You take it in turns to think of a subject – painters, scientists, musicians, soap operas, for example. Then everyone tries to find an example to go with each letter of the alphabet. You just say them out loud. There are no winners or losers in this game but it is interesting to see how much you know about different subjects.

Lists This requires a degree of mental agility and the use of pencil and paper, so it is best left until the end of the meal. The person at the head of the table writes down a letter, the person at the foot of the table writes down a subject, for example, aircraft. They simultaneously show what they have written to the other guests. Then for two minutes everyone writes down the names of aircraft beginning with that letter. The person with the most wins. The choice of subject and letter moves on clockwise round the table. You continue playing until one person has won as many times as there are guests, or you get bored.

Words

This is another variation on Lists. The first person thinks of a subject, for example, 'flowers'. The person clockwise then gives the name of a flower, for example, 'carnation'. The next person gives the name of a flower beginning with the last letter of the previous flower, in this case 'n'. 'Nasturtium' would do. This goes on until someone is unable to supply an answer. He or she then loses a point, and performs a forfeit. A simple game, but like croquet, provides tremendous scope for wickedness. By the way, the rotation of the game changes every time someone gets it wrong, so giving your neighbour a 'z' can have dire consequences.

The Worst Meal

You take it in turns to describe the worst meal you have ever had and why. Points are awarded arbitrarily for descriptive abilities, humour, horror and style. The winner is the one who is asked to leave the room. Our worst experience was our honeymoon at a famous West End hotel where Suzy got food poisoning from oysters (an occupational hazard for shellfish eaters, and no fault of the hotel) and was laid out for three days. They even tried to charge us for the doctor's bill! We will spare you the symptomatic details. When playing this game, it is usual to outlaw motorway service areas, railway stations, airports and cross-channel ferries from consideration, as their offerings do not usually fit into the category of food. This game can also be played as the 'Worst Journey', 'Worst Television Programme', 'Worst Play'. (We remember one where a much-gossiped-about actress's nether regions loomed out backwards from the stage, and one with the immortal line, 'You're not mad, but I am.') Or 'Worst Anything Else you can think of'.

Lateral Thinking Games

These can be extremely irritating or lots of fun; it depends on whether you are setting the problems or trying to guess them. The rules are simple: one person sets a problem such as: 'Two men go into a restaurant and order an albatross sandwich. They are served and each takes a bite from his sandwich. One is then happy, the other unhappy. Explain why.' The other guests then ask questions, to which the person answers yes, no, or irrelevant. The winner is the one who establishes what the story was. What makes the game interesting is that while there are always several different solutions that might fit, you have to find out the one the person has chosen. And, no, we're not going to tell you the solution to the 'albatross sandwich' problem.

Panel Games

There is nothing to stop you playing your favourite panel game (as long as it does not require special equipment). Good contenders are 'Just a minute', 'Call my Bluff' and 'Mornington Crescent'.

Alternative Trivia

This is a version of a popular series of games that does not require a board. Each guest is given a stack of question cards. Starting at the head of the table each person asks the person on their right questions from one card. This goes on until they get one wrong, in which case they ask the person on their right, or until someone answers a whole card's worth. The first person to do this is the winner.

The Psychology Game

This is the psychological equivalent of a newspaper's daily horoscope. Because of its nature you can only play this game once with any given set of people – they probably won't speak to you ever again. You ask your guests to imagine they are walking through a jungle. First they come to a clearing where they find a large, fierce looking tiger. Next they come to some water. When they've got past this, they come to the edge of the jungle and look out through the trees.

Get each guest to describe the jungle, what they did when they met the tiger, what happened with the water and what they saw at the edge of the jungle. You then tell them that the jungle represents what they think of their life at present, the tiger shows how they deal with problems, the water represents their attitude to sex, and what they saw at the jungle edge is how they see the future. There is tremendous scope for embarrassing analogy here. People who build a bridge over the water are in real trouble, as are those who drink it all. Those who feed their best friend to the tiger are almost certainly in politics, while those who live in pleasant designer jungles have obviously had no dealings with the Customs and Excise office yet. Have fun and use your imagination freely.

The Psychology Game II

Along similar lines to the above, but shorter. Get everyone to say what colour they would be, what sort of animal they would be and what sort of water they would be. They must give reasons for their choice. For example they might choose blue because it is the colour of the sky, and so on. The 'psychologist' then tells them that the colour reveals how they believe the world sees them, the animal shows how they see themselves and the water brings us back to sex again. A silly game but it does get people talking.

Desert (or Dessert) Island Alternatives

Instead of choosing eight favourite records, each guest chooses a subject. Everyone then says what their eight somethings would be and why. For example, cars, meals, drinks, countries, allergies, films, diseases. Use your imagination. As a variation, get people to choose the eight somethings they dislike most instead. It's the reasons that are the most fun.

Botticelli

This game has Victorian origins, or earlier for all we know. It has simple rules but can provide a tremendously high level of intellectual challenge, or out-trivialise the most ardent pursuer of trivia.

The head of the table starts first and chooses a letter, for example, 'N' and says 'I am an N' where N is the first letter of the character or object they have chosen to be. Going clockwise, each person can ask up to three questions such as: 'Are you a famous something?' where something is a scientist, painter, motorcar, aeroplane, household object, or whatever. The person who is 'it' has to answer with something which starts with the letter they have chosen and fits the category. For example, a famous scientist beginning with 'N' could be Newton.

If the person answers correctly then the questioner tries again, unless they have used up their three questions. Incidentally, within any one go you may only ask the same question three times. After that the next person starts again from scratch. You may only ask questions to which you know the answer. The victim may challenge you; if you do not know the answer yourself you are out of the game. If the person who is 'it' cannot answer correctly, then the questioner may ask a direct question such as 'Are you alive?', 'Are you fictional?', 'Are you a politician?' to which they must be given a correct answer.

This goes on until someone is able to guess the true identity of the person. You may guess at any time. However, if you guess incorrectly then you are out of the game until either the identity is guessed or a new game is started. The victor then chooses their own letter and the game begins anew, unless everyone is fed up with it, in which case have a glass of wine. If nobody guesses correctly then the first person has won and may start again with a different letter.

This is actually much easier than it sounds.

Murder Games　　There is a fashion for murder game kits. These are role-playing games where everyone takes a part in a sort of Agatha Christie play. The games are normally for eight or more people and involve pre-dinner drinks and snacks, a three-course meal and after dinner coffee and liqueurs. We have hosted a couple of these and they are great fun; they are also very hard work for the hosts. If you are to stand a chance of enjoying the game then it is vital that you organise yourself well in advance to sort the food out. The games usually come with a suggested menu; this normally requires a deal of preparation and cooking effort at the time of the meal. Consequently, you may find yourself running from pillar to post in an attempt to keep up. It is much easier to drop the formal meal in favour of a buffet. If you want to have something hot, then serve soup as a starter. This reduces the workload considerably and you may even have time to win the game.

Games for Children　　Young children can get very bored in the company of a lot of adults and it is worth having some simple games for them to play, either at or (preferably) away from the table to give the adults a chance. Jigsaw puzzles are a relatively safe game for the unsupervised. Avoid finger paints!

> "'Have you ever seen Spode eat asparagus?'
> 'No.'
> 'Revolting. It alters one's whole conception of Man as Natwe's last word.'"
>
> *P. G. Wodehouse*

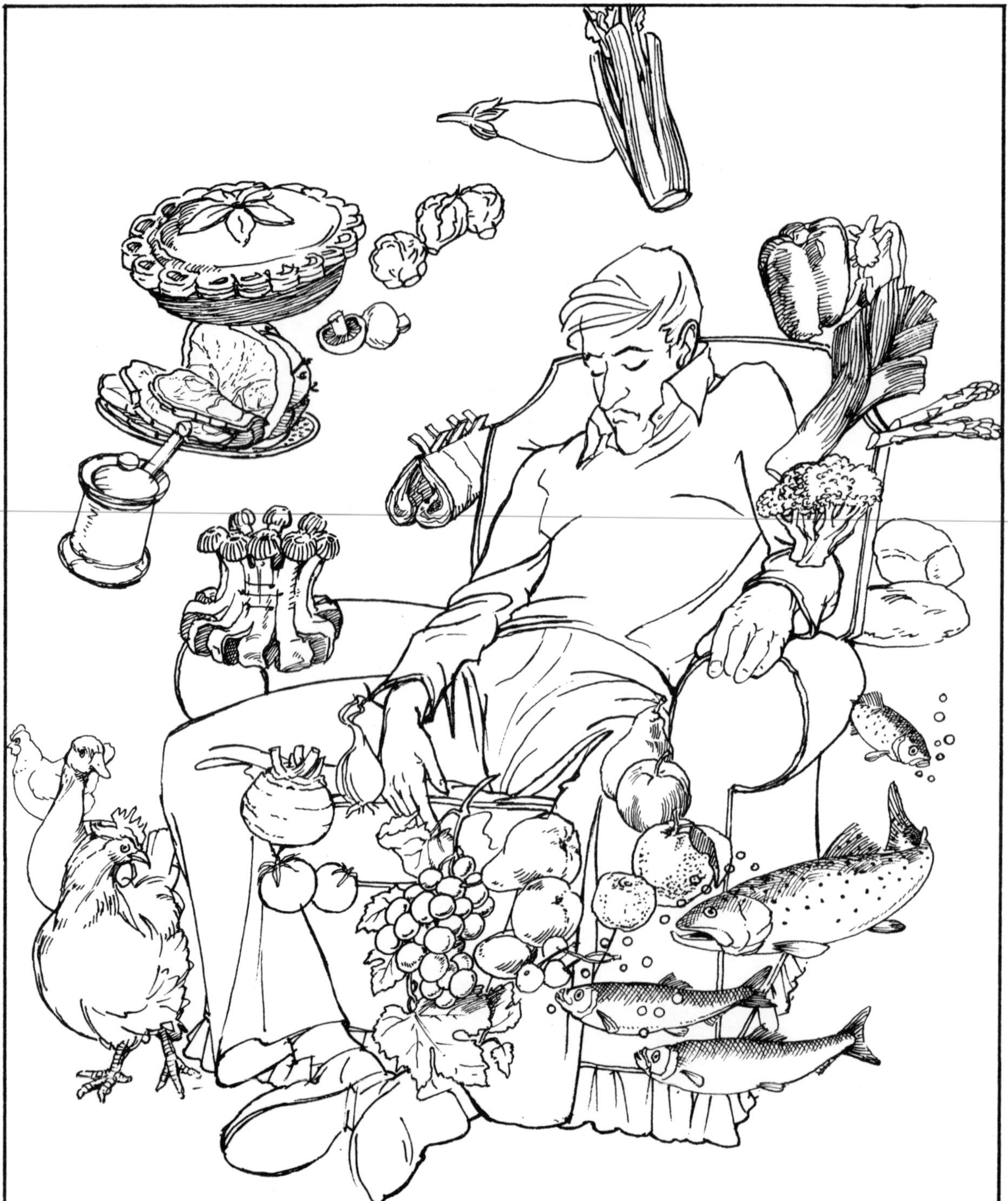

Chapter 10

Sunday Lunch
or
Weekend but Not Defeated

> **Traditionally the 'Roast Beef of Old England' but Lamb, Pork or Chicken are just as good (the latter being suitable for the 'Vegetarian, but we do eat fish and chicken, as long as it's free-range of course' brigade). This is one of the hardest meals to do well; our mothers knew how but a lot of the present generation have passed it by. It is amazing how many cooks can produce amazing exotica such as Chicken stuffed with prunes in lemon sauce on a bed of anchovies (Yuk!), but are reduced to a quivering heap by a Sunday lunch.**

We think that a good Sunday lunch has two courses, the main one of roast meat, and, after a suitable gap, the pudding/cheese event. Maybe, after the guests have slept the worst of it off we might provide drop scones, raspberry jam and butter for high tea. This may not be healthy but it is a most relaxing way to spend a Sunday, particularly a wet one. If the guests are incapable of motion by the end of the afternoon, then you have succeeded.

Brunch   This is an American idea. You eat it at about eleven o'clock, and it has one major advantage over Sunday lunch, at least for the activity conscious. You can get it all over with before one o'clock and have the rest of the day free to go out and about. Sunday lunch does tend to occupy most of the day, and the after-effects have been known to carry on well into the evening. Brunch covers a multitude of sins, but on the odd occasions that we've indulged in it, this is what we've served.

Waffles (hot) with a choice of apricot jam, golden syrup or honey.

Grilled bacon, scrambled eggs, fried mushrooms, fried bread, fried tomatoes.

Toast and marmalade, or on its own.

Tea, coffee, fruit juice, tomato juice, cold beer.

Traditional Sunday Lunches

(I've lost count of how many Sunday lunches we have shovelled into him. – S.)

(I am convinced that his bachelor days are numbered. A man in possession of a reasonable income, a good kitchen and the ability to produce Sunday lunch must be in need of a wife. – S.)

More so than for almost any other meal, planning is king for a roast with all the trimmings. A bachelor friend of ours has just had his kitchen and dining room furbished. He has only been in the house for about eight years and had totally ignored this area of the property, working on the principle that he always ate at restaurants or with friends and so the kitchen didn't matter too much. It looked as though several Harley Davidson motorcycles were being built in it. This was somewhat strange as our friend doesn't own any form of transport other than shoes. However, persuasion based on flattery ('Anyone who appreciates food so much must have the makings of a wonderful cook') has produced results and we were the first guests for Sunday lunch produced in the new kitchen. Being of a technical bent he solved the planning problem by using a 'bar chart'. The results of this foray into the complex world of the Sunday lunch were impressive, so we've included an example of his method for other ingénue cooks.

The idea is to extend the normal planning activities by the adoption of scientific method!

The diagram shows a bar chart for cooking roast beef and Yorkshire pudding with roast potatoes, carrots, peas and gravy.

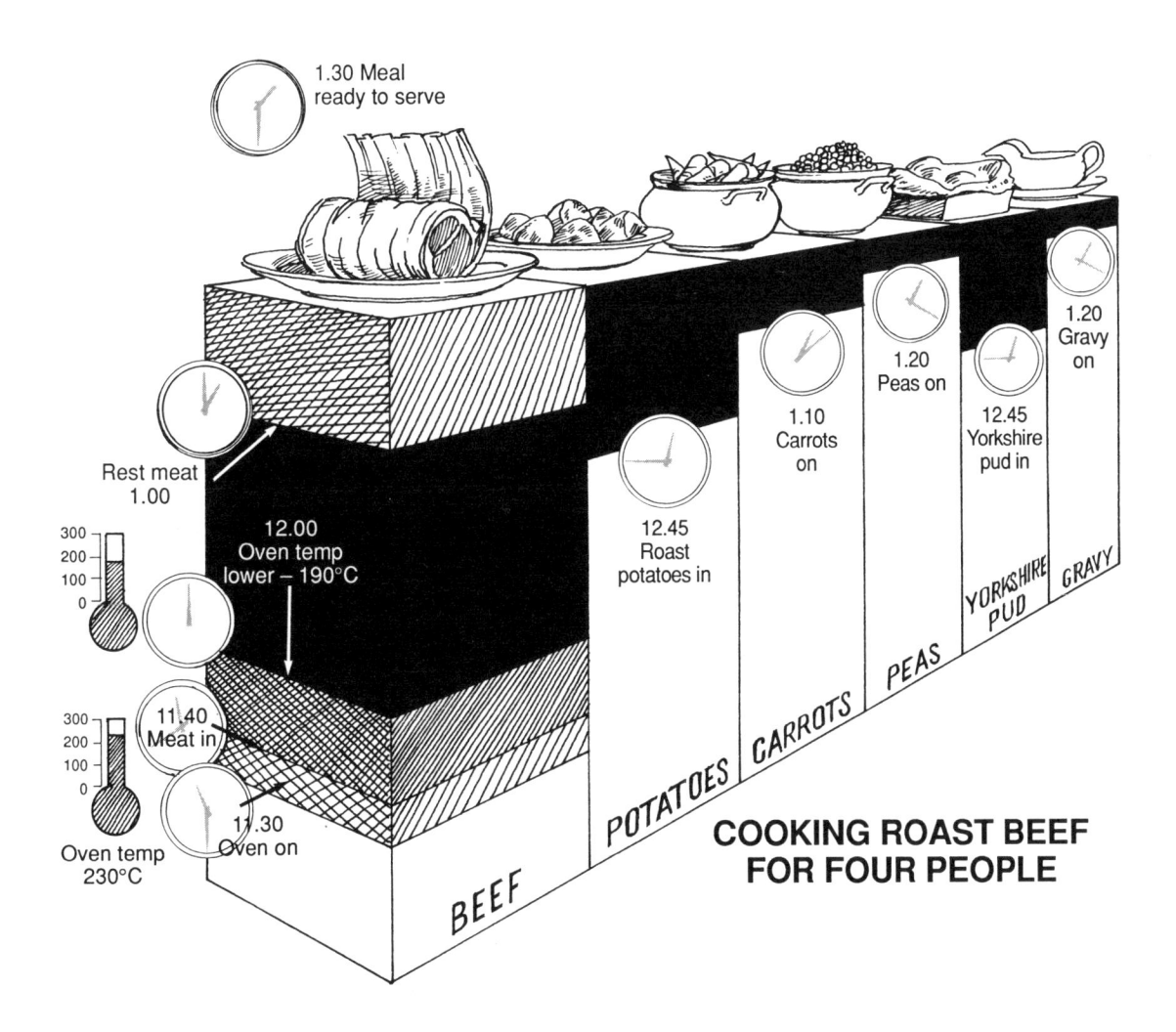

COOKING ROAST BEEF FOR FOUR PEOPLE

1.30 Meal ready to serve

Rest meat 1.00

12.00 Oven temp lower – 190°C

11.40 Meat in

11.30 Oven on

Oven temp 230°C

12.45 Roast potatoes in

1.10 Carrots on

1.20 Peas on

12.45 Yorkshire pud in

1.20 Gravy on

BEEF · POTATOES · CARROTS · PEAS · YORKSHIRE PUD · GRAVY

It works like this. Decide when you are going to serve the meal then calculate everything backwards from that. For example, the meat will take the longest time to cook, in this case a four pound joint will take 1 hour 40 minutes to roast and then should have 20 minutes to rest. The oven takes, say, 20 minutes to reach temperature, so you have to start the whole thing off 2 hours 20 minutes before serving time. You apply the same principle to things like peas and carrots, always working backwards from the serving time. You then draw a vertical line on the right hand side of a piece of paper to represent the finishing time and draw horizontal lines from right to left with length in proportion to the time needed for cooking. A scale of 3 inches (8 centimetres) to the hour should be about right. This will leave you with a nice chart, with times on it which tell you what to do when.

This method really does work, even for the raw beginner, and is much less laborious than it sounds. However, once you've done a few Sunday lunches you won't need to do things this way; you'll find it just happens naturally.

Sunday 'Guz-with'

Roast Potatoes *(Preparation and cooking time, 40 to 50 mins)*

Method

Always use 'old' potatoes for this. Simply peel, cut and dry the potatoes (use kitchen roll), score them lightly with a fork and dust with flour (and optionally herbs). Place in the roasting pan if you already have a joint of meat cooking at over 200°C/400°F/gas mark 6 for the last 40 minutes of the roasting. If cooking them on their own, then preheat the oven to that temperature and cook in vegetable oil for 40 minutes turning them occasionally.

Roast Parsnips *(Preparation and cooking time, 40 to 50 mins)*

Method
Peel and dry the parsnips then treat as for potatoes with the exception of the flour.

Yorkshire Pudding *(Preparation and cooking time, 50 mins)*

This is the most important 'guz-with' as far as roast beef is concerned and must be done well if the meal is to be a success.

Ingredients
4 oz/125 gm plain flour
¼ pint/150 ml water
¼ pint/150 ml milk
1 egg
pinch of salt

Method
Sift the flour and salt into a bowl. Mix the milk and water. Use a wooden spoon to mix the egg and 2 tablespoons (30 ml) of liquid into a quarter of the dry ingredients until you get a smooth paste. Then mix in the remainder of the liquid and the flour, a little at a time, to make a smooth and frothy batter. Add an ice cube to the mixture and allow it to melt before you start cooking the batter. Make sure the oven is up to 220°C/425°F/gas mark 7 and place a little lard in the bottom of shallow baking tins/special Yorkshire pudding tins and place in the oven. When the fat has melted, remove the tins from the oven, pour in the mixture and return to the oven for 40 minutes. Try not to open the oven until cooking is complete, though this may be unavoidable. If you are cooking roast beef (and you probably are), then turn up the oven (it will be at 190°C/375°F/gas mark 5) 15 minutes before the beef is due to come out and start the Yorkshire cooking straight away. It can then finish off whilst the meat is resting.

Mint Sauce *(Preparation and cooking time 5 mins)*

How do you worry sheep? Run after them shouting 'Mint Sauce! Mint Sauce!' Ho-Ho.

Ingredients

sprig of fresh mint
2 teaspoons sugar
1 tablespoon boiling water
1 fl oz/25 ml vinegar

Method

Wash and chop the mint leaves. Put the sugar in the sauceboat and add the boiling water. Stir to dissolve, then add the mint and the vinegar. *Et voilà!*

Apple Sauce *(Preparation time 10 mins)*

Commonly served with roast pork, but not always by us, I don't know why.

Ingredients

1 cooking apple
3 fl oz/100 ml water
cinnamon (optional)

Method

Couldn't be easier. Simply peel and dice the apple and simmer in the water until you have the sauce. Add cinnamon if you like that sort of thing.

Bread Sauce *(Preparation and cooking time 30 to 40 mins)*

This is perfect with roast chicken and roast pork.

Ingredients

cloves
½ oz/10 gm butter
1 large onion
¾ pint/400 ml milk
3 oz/75 gm fresh breadcrumbs
salt and pepper

Method

Cut the onion up into fairly small pieces then add it to the cloves and milk in a saucepan and simmer for 20 minutes. Allow to cool, then add the breadcrumbs, butter, salt and pepper and reheat. You should get a nice thick sauce which can be used hot or cold.

Sage and Onion Stuffing

(Preparation time 10 mins, cooking time 40 mins upwards)

This traditional stuffing is much underrated, mainly because too many people serve that packet stuff. Do not do that! It doesn't take very long to do it right.

Ingredients

2 large onions
2 teaspoons dried sage (or chopped fresh if you can get it)
1 oz/25 gm butter
4 oz/110 gm fresh breadcrumbs
salt and pepper

Method

Finely chop the onions and cook in boiling water until soft. Drain and throw away the water. Mix the onions with the other ingredients in a bowl until it sticks together fairly well. Cook with pork or fowl. On its own allow 40 minutes in a hot oven; inside a bird it takes as long as the bird. When cooking it separately, check from time to time to ensure that it does not get overcooked or burnt.

Variation: If you are going to stuff a chicken with this, then it is a nice addition to mix in the finely chopped liver of the chicken with the breadcrumbs; this will give additional flavour and moisture to the meal.

Sunday 'Guz-in-the-Middles'

Lamb

(Preparation and cooking time, typically 2½ hours)

When pricked with generous quantities of fresh rosemary and garlic, roast English lamb becomes positively continental. It is not such a heavy meal as beef and leaves you with a better chance of being able to move afterwards, which gives you more scope for high tea.

Ingredients

leg of lamb
garlic
honey
rosemary

Method

Preheat the oven to 175°C/350°F/gas mark 4. Use a sharp knife to make slits in the surface of the lamb and fill these with slivers of garlic or rosemary leaves. Glaze with honey. Roast in the oven for 20 minutes per

Guz-with
roast potatoes
French beans
carrots
redcurrant jelly
mint sauce

pound, then rest for 15 to 20 minutes before serving. Deglacé the fat in the pan with sherry or red wine to make the gravy. Add stock and reduce to the required thickness.

Beef *(Preparation and cooking time, typically 2½ to 3 hours)*

As traditionally British as you can get, it is still the king of Sunday roasts, especially in winter. Rib of beef is the preferred choice, though it is really suitable for serving six or more people. For smaller gatherings sirloin or topside joints may be more suitable.

Ingredients

rib of beef (allow at least ½ lb/225 gm per person)
Dijon mustard
olive oil
sherry

Guz-with

Yorkshire pudding
roast potatoes
roast parsnips
Brussels sprouts
carrots

Method

Preheat the oven to 230°C/450°F/gas mark 8. Coat the rib all over with the mustard and dribble a little oil over the joint. Put in the oven and cook for 20 minutes at the initial temperature. Reduce the temperature to 190°C/375°F/gas mark 5 and cook for a further 20 minutes per pound. Then rest the joint at room temperature (cover with silver foil) for between 15 minutes and half an hour. This will give you scope for solving any timing problems with the vegetables prior to serving. Deglacé the residue in the roasting pan with sherry to make the gravy.

Serve with all the trimmings and allow a large gap before the pudding. Any good Bordeaux or Burgundy wine will do nicely with this meal.

Pork *(Preparation and cooking time, typically 2 to 2½ hours)*

This is Suzy's speciality. With pork it's the accessories that make the meal; the stuffing, the apple sauce, the roast potatoes and the crackling are what it's all about. Nobody makes crackling like our Suzy; you can really 'pig-out' on it.

Ingredients
joint of pork
oil
flaked salt (preferably sea salt)
Guz-with stuffing
apple sauce
roast potatoes
peas or French beans

Method
Preheat the oven to 200°C/400°F/gas mark 6. Make the stuffing. Before you roast the joint, dry it thoroughly with paper towels, dribble a teaspoonful of vegetable oil over it and then rub a very large pinch of flaked sea salt into the rind until your fingertips go pink with the effort. Place in a roasting pan and cook in the oven for 25 minutes per pound on the bone, 30 minutes for rolled joints, plus 25 minutes, again 30 minutes if a rolled joint, to finish. It is very important to make sure that pork is properly cooked all the way through.

To make the gravy, pour off most of the fat out of the roasting pan and deglacé the residue with dry vermouth. Thicken with a little gravy browning, adding stock if required for quantity.

Chicken *(Preparation and cooking time, typically 2 hours)*

When you don't feel like red meat, chicken makes an excellent meal. For roasting, either get a good free-range bird, or a corn-fed one. Nothing else has enough flavour to be worth cooking. You can have red or white wine with this, so it's a good Sunday lunch for guests with a preference for white wine.

Ingredients
1 chicken
2 oz/50 gm butter
6 rashers of streaky bacon
[For the alternative method you will need 20 garlic cloves.]

Guz-with

stuffing, sage and onion or oranges and lemons
bread sauce
roast potatoes
peas

Method
Preheat the oven to 200°C/400°F/gas mark 6. Remove the giblets from the bird and reserve for making the gravy. Rinse out the chicken with cold water. Stuff the bird with either sage and onion stuffing or with slices of orange and lemon.

Baste the bird with butter and lard with the bacon – this means cover the bird with strips of bacon. Put into a roasting tin and cook in the oven for 20 minutes per pound plus 20 minutes to finish. Note the timings are given for stuffed birds, empty ones take less. It is as well to check by pushing a skewer into the bird's breast and thighs to see if blood runs out. If it does, then more cooking is needed.

Boil the giblets for half an hour (you can do this any time whilst the chicken is roasting) and add the liquid to the roasting pan (with its juices) after removing the chicken. Reduce this to make the gravy and season to taste.

An alternative method of roasting chicken is to cook the chicken as described above but resting on a bed of 20 garlic cloves (uncrushed). This is not as horrendous as it sounds. You don't eat these cloves, but their flavours will rise and permeate the chicken. The result is wonderful and much less garlicky than Chicken Kiev. Do give it a try.

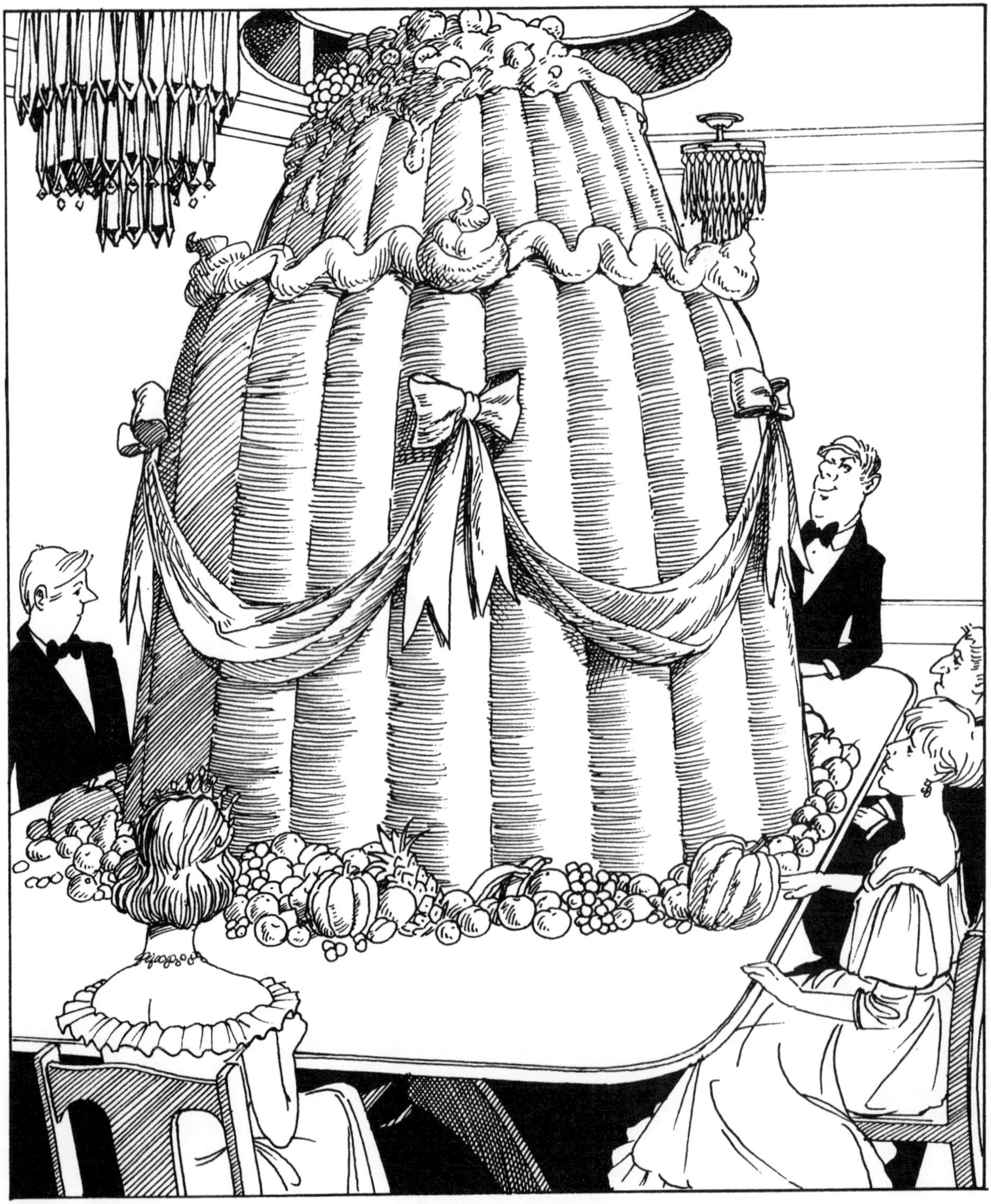

Chapter 11

Stodgy Puddings
or
Wealth Food Not Health Food

> **The lid has been blown off *nouvelle cuisine*; the 1980s saw the resurgence of wealth food in place of health food; let's make the nineties even naughtier. Sensible-sized portions are with us again. One of the best things about this is the resurgence of the Pudding. Here are the basic techniques and a few fun recipes. Puddings do not have to be thought of as wicked and sinful (though that is half the fun). One of the best New Year's Day meals we had was steamed ginger pudding and Sauterne – nothing else. It was a real treat.**

Puddings come in two main categories – those to be eaten hot and those to be eaten cold. For serving, 'Hot with custard, Cold with cream, Makes your cooking go a dream'. This awful rhyme will remain mercifully anonymous but is a reasonable guideline. Where we think a pudding should be served contrary to this rule, we have said so in the recipe. These traditional puddings are time-consuming affairs and should not be attempted unless you have time and to spare.

Note: The recipes in this chapter serve six people unless a different number is specified in the text. However, this is dependent on the greed of the individuals concerned.

Hot Stuff

Aunty Marmalade's Steamed Ginger Pudding

(Preparation time 15 mins, cooking time 2 hours)

This recipe makes a pudding to beat all puddings. It is so good that men have been known to propose marriage to its creator on the spot (regardless of their own girlfriends/fiancées/wives). The recipe serves from 4 to 8 people, depending how large their appetites are.

Ingredients

6 oz/175 gm fresh breadcrumbs
4 oz/110 gm suet
4 oz/110 gm Demerara sugar
2 tablespoons golden syrup
1 teaspoon ground ginger
1 teaspoon baking powder
1 teaspoon plain flour
1 egg
a little milk
butter for greasing bowl

Method

Mix the baking powder with the flour. In a large mixing bowl blend the breadcrumbs, sugar and ginger. Next add all the dry ingredients. Stir in the syrup followed by the egg. When this has reached an even consistency, add a little milk to bind the mixture together (never more than a quarter of a cup). Grease a Pyrex or similar pudding basin with butter. Put mixture into the bowl and cover with kitchen foil. Place the bowl in a pan of water and steam for 2 hours with the lid on the pan. Make sure you do not let the pan boil dry! Serve with real custard or cream. Aunty Marmalade says that hot golden syrup is even better – in fact she described it as orgasmic – but we worried in case that would offend the readers. You aren't offended, are you? Of course not.

Spotted Dick

(Preparation time 15 mins, cooking time 3 hours)

Reminiscent of school dinners, lumpy custard and an overwhelming odour of institutional cabbage, this is nevertheless a pudding of quality.

Ingredients

4 oz/110 gm self-raising flour
4 oz/110 gm shredded suet
4 oz/110 gm white breadcrumbs (slightly stale)
4 oz/110 gm dried currants or sultanas
butter
brown sugar
water

Method

Mix all the dried ingredients together in a mixing bowl with a fork or a spoon. Add a little water and mix into a dough. Flour a board and shape the dough into a roll. Cover the roll with greaseproof paper and aluminium foil. Steam the pudding using the same method as for **Aunty Marmalade's Steamed Ginger Pudding** for 2½ to 3 hours. Serve with butter and brown sugar, or with custard if you prefer.

Bread and Butter Pudding

(Preparation time 30 mins, cooking time 45 mins)

Not to be confused with bread pudding, this is one of the all time greats of the pudding club. Loved by children and adults alike, it reaches parts of the belly that other puddings cannot reach.

Ingredients

½ pint/300 ml milk
2 oz/50 gm sultanas or dried currants
2 eggs
3 oz/75 gm caster sugar
3–4 drops vanilla essence
ground nutmeg
slices of bread (slightly stale)
butter

Method

Pre-heat the oven to 175°C/350°F/gas mark 4 and butter a deep bowl. Beat the eggs whilst bringing the milk almost to the boil. Pour the hot milk over the eggs, stirring all the while, and add in the vanilla essence. Butter the bread and cut the slices in half. Place a layer of buttered slices in the bottom of the bowl and cover them with currants and sugar. Repeat this until you have got to the top of the dish (just put sugar on the top layer). Then pour in the egg custard until it is just below the top layer. Dot with butter and sprinkle with nutmeg. Cook in the oven for 45 minutes and serve hot.

Apple Crumble

(Preparation time 20 mins, cooking time 25 mins)

A good crumble should stick closer than a brother. There has to be a certain degree of sticky gooeyness if it is to be a success.

Ingredients

1 lb/450 gm apples
6 oz/175 gm plain flour
6 oz/175 gm caster sugar
3 oz/75 gm margarine
1 teaspoon cinnamon
¼ pint/150ml water

Method

Preheat the oven to 175°C/350°F/gas mark 4. Peel, core and cut the apples into small pieces and stew for 10 to 15 minutes in the water. Rub the margarine into the flour and half the sugar until it achieves the texture of breadcrumbs. Add the rest of the sugar and mix well. Put the stewed fruit into the bottom of an ovenproof dish and mix in the cinnamon. Spread the mixture over the top of this and place in the oven for 20 to 25 minutes. Serve hot with real custard.

Real Custard *(Preparation time 5 mins, cooking time 10 mins upwards)*

Real custard is vastly superior to that powder-based stuff and it need not take much longer to make. The thicker you want the custard the longer you need to cook it, though there are limits on how thick you can make it.

Ingredients

7 fl oz/200 ml milk
7 fl oz/200 ml double cream
2 egg yolks
1 oz/25 gm caster sugar

Method

Beat the eggs and the sugar together in a mixing bowl with a fork or a balloon whisk until smooth. Mix the milk and cream together in a saucepan and bring gently to the boil. When the mixture gets to the boil take it off the heat and mix in the egg/sugar mixture. Return to a low heat and stir continuously until it has thickened. If you want to make the custard more or less rich, try varying the proportions of milk and cream, but keep the total amount of liquid about the same. Serve hot. If you want to make it earlier, then keep it warm in a basin over simmering water and stir frequently to prevent a skin forming.

Cold Stuff

Summer Pudding *(Preparation time 30 mins, standing time 8 hours)*

This is the best way known to mankind to use up stale bread and excess summer fruits. It is fantastic when served with double cream.

Ingredients (quantities depend on size of bowl)

blackberries, raspberries, strawberries (chopped), redcurrants
thin-sliced stale bread

Method

This is very easy to do but has to be done the previous day/evening. Destalk and wash the fruit. Line a pudding basin (heatproof) with the slices of bread; you may have to cut them to shape to achieve a good fit. Dissolve the sugar in the water by boiling, add the fruit

sugar (typically 5 oz/150 gm)
water (typically ¼ pint/150 ml)

and simmer for 10 to 15 minutes depending on the fruit. Pour the mixture into the lined basin and cover the top with more sliced bread. Put a plate over the top of this and weight down. Leave until cool (an hour or two), then transfer to the refrigerator. Leave overnight. Remove from refrigerator 30 minutes before required and turn out onto a plate to serve. The pudding should have a beautiful pink and red marbled look to it.

Charlotte Russe *(Preparation time 2 hours, chilling time 1 hour)*

It is extremely rare to find a real Charlotte Russe served in a restaurant. This is a pity because it is a real treat of a pudding. It is most definitely not one for the diet conscious amongst us.

Ingredients

Custard
5 fl oz/150 ml cream
5 fl oz/150 ml milk
2 egg yolks
½ oz/10 gm caster sugar

Charlotte Russe
½ packet of red or yellow jelly cubes
fresh raspberries
fresh or glacé cherries
¼ pint/150 ml double cream
½ oz/10 gm gelatine
1 fl oz/25 ml water
1 packet sponge fingers (or enough to line the basin)
Cointreau (or sherry if you prefer)

Method

First make the custard using the directions for **Real Custard** given earlier in this chapter, but using the quantities given here. Allow the custard to go cold; this will take an hour or so.

Then make enough jelly (follow manufacturer's directions) to fill the bottom ¼ inch/1 cm of a basin/mould. Pour in and allow to set. Wash and mix the fruit and put it into the basin. Cover with jelly and allow to set. Make up the rest of the jelly and use while still liquid to coat the sponge fingers. Line a pudding basin with upright coated sponge fingers and allow to set in position. Whip the cream together with the cold custard and the Cointreau. Melt the gelatine in 1 fl oz/25 ml of hot water and stir into the mixture. Pour the mixture into the lined basin and chill for at least one hour.

To serve, tip out onto a flat plate and let everyone admire it. If it falls apart serve it in the kitchen.

Home-made Chocolates

These are easy to do and what little effort is spent is amply repaid by your guests' appreciation.

Ingredients

white, milk or plain cooking chocolate
fresh fruit, such as strawberries
dried fruit
shelled, non-salted nuts
rum, whisky, brandy

Method

The simplest and possibly the nicest chocolate to make is a dipped strawberry. Just melt some plain or white chocolate (milk chocolate is a bit too wishy-washy for our taste). Take a strawberry and holding it by the stalk (hands up those who have already destalked theirs), dip it into the liquid chocolate. Hold it in the air for a while until it is set and transfer to the refrigerator.

> "Why, you might just as well say that 'I see what I eat' is the same thing as 'I eat what I see'!"
> *Lewis Carroll*

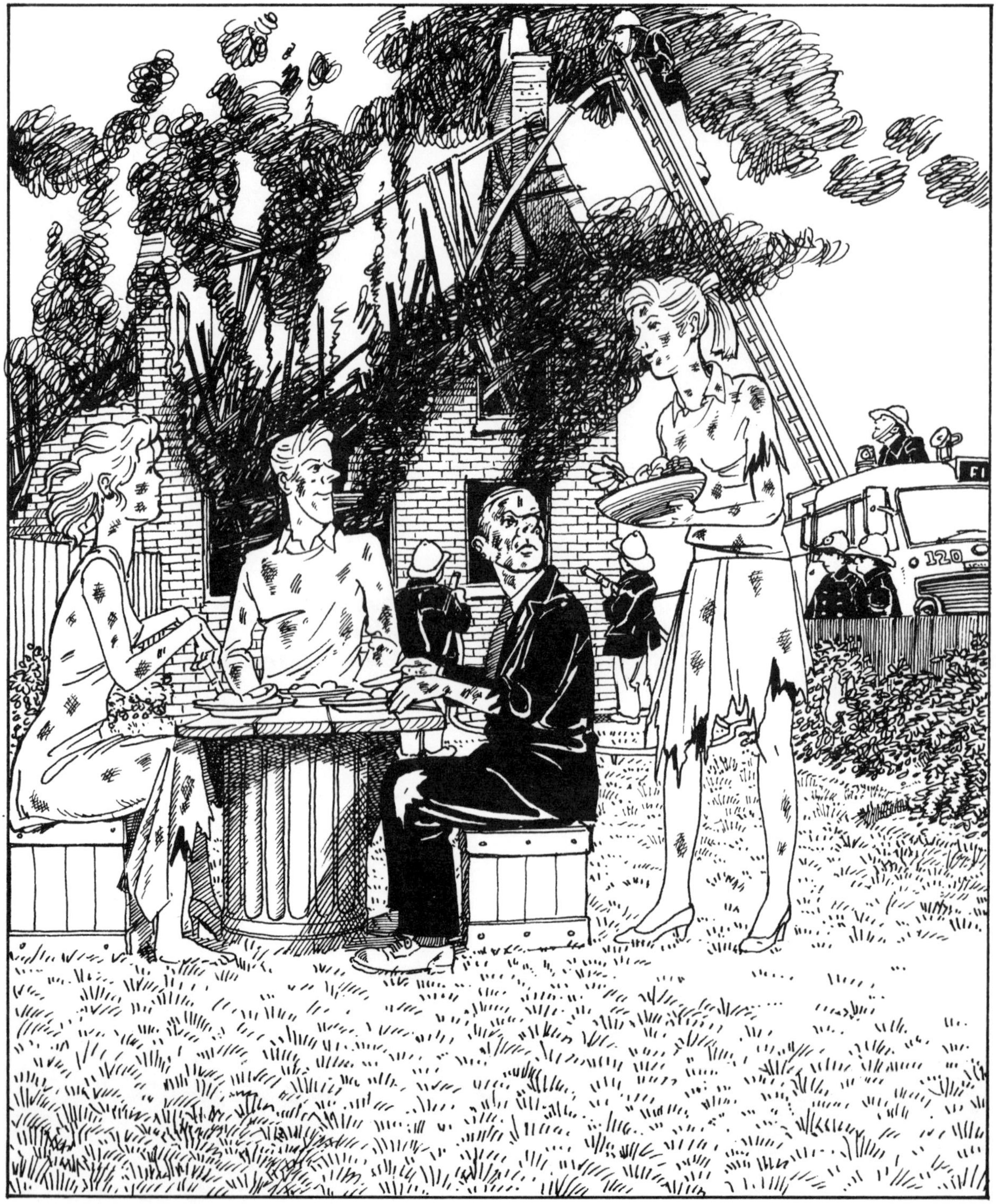
120

Chapter 12

Disasters and How to Recover from Them
or
There's Many a Slip Twixt the Cup and the Dry Cleaners

> **It is amazing how many disasters can befall even the best organised dinner party. They vary from the mundane red wine on the white dress to the house next door collapsing in the gale.**

Setting fire to the kitchen This is a tricky one. Our Appendix B tells you how to put out the fire or when to call the fire brigade. However, unless the fire is very minor, the smell will be appalling even if the kitchen is still serviceable. Unless the dining room/drawing room are well away from the smell, the best thing is to greet your guests and withdraw gracefully with them to the nearest restaurant you can get in at. You can clean up later.

Power cuts During the meal, it is just a matter of lighting candles and doing the best you can. Earlier on, it is a major problem unless you're cooking with gas. Then all you need is candles for a wonderful evening in the face of adversity. However, if you're all electric it's down to the restaurant or make do with cheese, salad, cold meats (cooked, not raw) and whatever you've got for dessert. Try and recreate the blitz spirit and you'll be OK.

Equipment failure

With the exception of the refrigerator and the rings, most things can be coped with; at least they can be with a bit of ingenuity. Admittedly this can mean that you have to change to steaks or a stew instead of a roast. For example, the blender can be replaced with combinations of grater, sieves and sharp knives. Most alternatives require large amounts of work – that is why Victorian kitchens had to have so many staff. You could try press-ganging the guests into helping. You can also try the beg, steal or borrow approach with your friends.

Armageddon

Arm a geddon out of here? Not much that you can do about this one except ask St Peter how he likes his steaks cooked as you take the down elevator. This one can ruin your whole universe.

Unexpurgated (sorry, unexpected guests)

There are a number of solutions to this disaster. *One*, get rid of them – boiling oil, mimicking the symptoms of severe food poisoning, hiding behind the sofa and pretending to be out or anything else you can think up. *Two*, take them round to the local restaurant/Chinese/Indian, particularly useful if it is your fault. *Three*, magic something up: Spaghetti Carbonara is easy and quick and you probably have the ingredients (eggs, bacon/ham, cream, garlic, pasta) in stock anyway. Serve cheese or fruit for a pudding and give them lots to drink – they'll never notice. If all else fails, resort to the recipes given under the heading **Unexpected Starter, Main Course, Dessert**.

Boring guests

These can be difficult to remove, particularly if they are customers. Conversation stoppers such as 'Dahling, are you sure the doctor said that it was all right for you to prepare the salad with your skin condition?' or 'My God, I left Granny on the Circle line; do you think she's still going round?' are the sort of thing in these circumstances. Another good ploy in a big city is to have your partner break some small glass object in another room while you tell them how awful the car break-ins are getting. 'Did you remember to lock yours up? It's not in XYZ Street (the only one nearby with parking spaces) is it?'

Guests who are early People travelling by public transport or making long journeys often build in so much spare time to deal with possible hold-ups that they are early. Other people just don't look at their watches often enough. As a result you may get guests turning up an hour or so before time. The hospitable solution is to ask them into the kitchen to talk and have a drink whilst you sort things out. This is a mistake – two people in one kitchen is fine, but three or four is more than a crowd – it's a disaster. The best thing to do is to sit them down in the drawing room, ask them to choose and put on some music, give them a drink, make them as comfortable as possible and get on with the cooking. One or other of you can pop out of the kitchen and chat during the quiet moments. The time will soon pass and nobody need get flustered. If they are so early that you're still in the bath, then there's not a lot you can do short of telling them to take a stroll to the local pub and come back later. Do this tactfully if you can.

Guests who are late This depends on how late they are and whether or not they have told you what time they will arrive. Half an hour late is usually just an inconvenience, an hour or more usually means that you have a problem, unless they told you in advance that this was going to happen. In the case where some guests are on time and only one or two are late, then you just have to feed them a few savoury nibblies and keep the apéritif sessions going a bit longer until they arrive. You should be able to put most things back by turning down the oven and not putting the vegetables on until it's time. There comes a point when you can no longer do this, it being unfair to the other guests. Then you should go ahead and run it like a theatre. If they turn up late they join in at the start of the next course. If it's only pudding, tough.

Hint: Do not put the vegetables on (except roast) until the guests have arrived. These can then cook during the chitchat and first course, and you only have to worry about the meat.

Guests who don't turn up

Not much can be done to salvage this except feed those who do come with extra food and use the rest up for such things as shepherd's pie, cottage pie, making stock or what have you. If all your guests fail to arrive, make sure you've got the right evening. If you have, curse and swear a lot and have a candlelit dinner for two. Puddings and starters will often not have been made up at this stage and their ingredients can be salvaged for another day. Likewise the vegetables can be kept for the next day's use.

Unexpected vegetarians

Again you're in real trouble here, unless you're vegetarian yourself. The best thing to do is keep some suitable ready-to-cook vegetarian meal in stock; many supermarkets and delicatessens do them. If you have a freezer, keep a vegetable curry for these occasions.

Teetotal

This is often encountered, especially if one or other of your guests has to drive. Just keep a stock of fruit juice, designer water (lime juice goes well with this), tomato juice and other similar beverages.

Food poisoning

This will never happen. At least if you follow the rules given in Appendix B, it shouldn't. If they arrive with this problem, send them home to bed or point them at the bathroom. Be sympathetic.

Hangovers

Generally these are not a problem until some time after the dinner party. However, if you are suffering from one from the night before, we offer this advice. Drink lots of fluid, preferably fruit juice cut fifty-fifty with still mineral water, take one of those fizzy vitamin tablets that give you a large (1 gm) dose of vitamin C. Better still, take one that supplies vitamin B as well. Eat or drink something sweet and get some fresh air. Lie down whenever you feel the need and let nature take its course. With luck you should recover within three to four hours.

Note: Do not drive for at least twenty-four hours – you will probably still be too drunk to be safe.

Hint: Hangover avoidance. Method A, don't drink too much. Method B, drink as much water as you possibly can (a pint or two is about right) just before you go to bed, and have water by your bed in case you wake up thirsty. This should minimise the after-effects.

Inappropriate dress For example, you said formal and two of the guests misunderstood and have come informal, in jeans. Worse still, they've come in fancy dress and you meant it to be casual (though how a mistake like this occurs is beyond our imagination. More likely they just have a warped sense of humour). There is only one solution to this problem – ignore it with true British phlegm and pretend that nothing has happened.

Spillages This covers a multitude of sins – the most common being spilled wine, cream and gravy. The table below suggests cures for these problems. The golden rule is not to panic; nothing is ever so awful that it need be the end of the evening, and swift but unhurried action will usually prevent permanent damage.

Stain	*Action*
White wine	Soak immediately with sparkling mineral water and clean up with a sponge and/or paper kitchen towels.

Red wine	The most common stain – at least our guests seem to spill a fair amount of the stuff. Treat as for white wine. Pouring salt on top of freshly spilt wine does soak up a lot of the wine, but often leaves a residual mark.
Chocolate	Soak in cold water for over half an hour, then rub with neat detergent and rinse clean. Non-washables should be dry-cleaned.
Fruit	Sponge straight away with cold water only. If non-washable, dry-clean; if washable rinse with very hot water.
Gravy	Sponge with cold water then wash or dry-clean as appropriate for the material.
Tea and coffee	If the material is washable, stretch it over a bowl and secure with elastic, then pour boiling water through the stain. Wash as normal. Non-washables should be sponged with water, then salt poured on top to soak up the stain. Allow to dry and brush or vacuum off gently.
Candle wax	Remove as much as you can with a knife. Then cover the area with paper towels and apply a warm iron to soak up the remainder.
Milk and cream	If the material is washable, just wash it in the normal way. If it is not, sponge with cold water and sprinkle with salt to soak up the stain and brush or vacuum off gently.
Mustard	If washable, rub with liquid detergent and rinse, then wash in the normal way. If not washable, dry-clean.
Cigarettes	These are not necessarily a disaster in themselves, but they can lead to burns in the tablecloth, sofa and clothing. All of these irritations can be quelled by

slinging some water, or white wine if you haven't any water to hand, on the site of the problem. Messier than this is the overturned ashtray. If this happens do not try and clean up with a damp cloth – the result of combining ash with water is an amazingly powerful staining agent. Use a vacuum cleaner or a dustpan and brush.

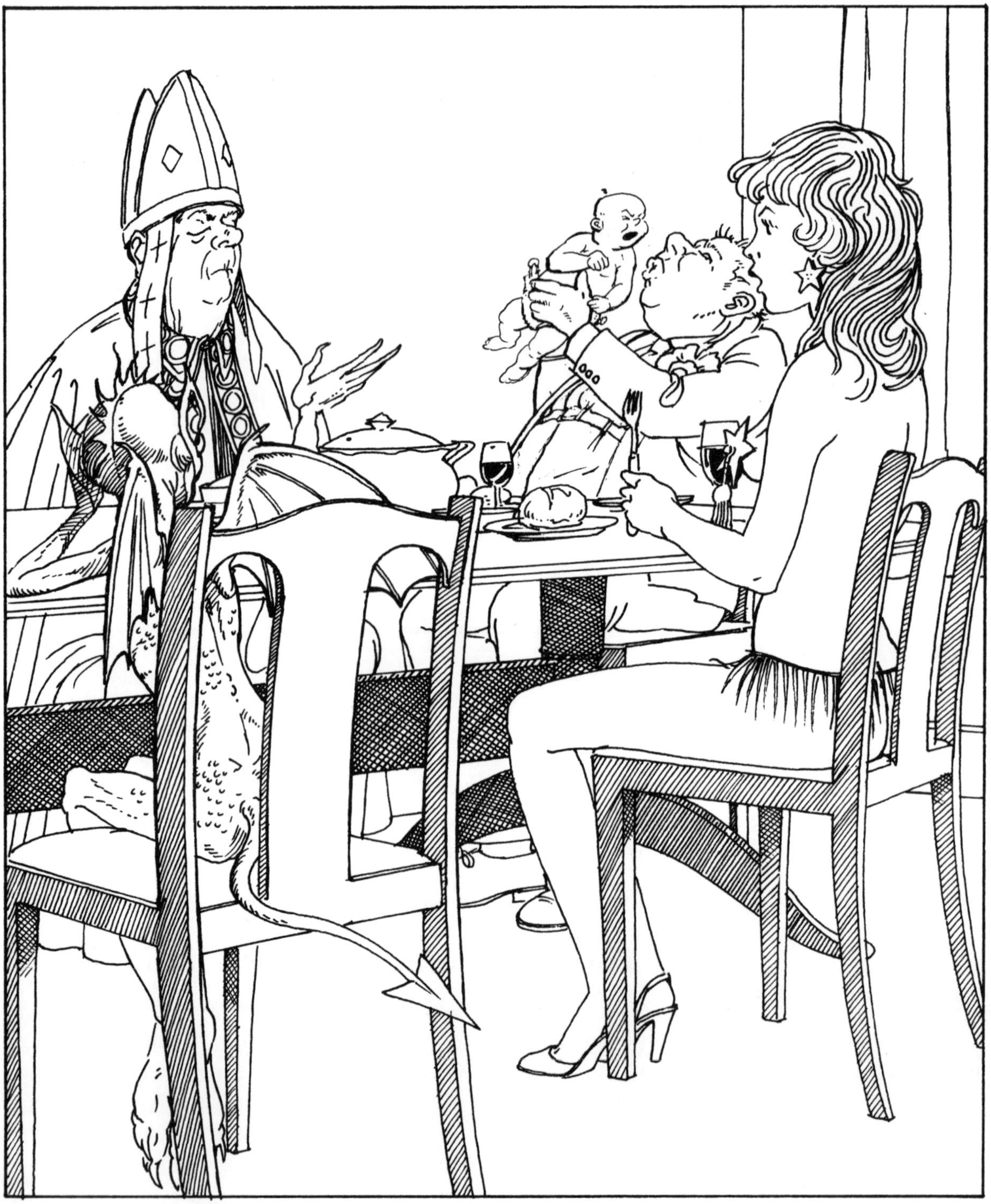

Chapter 13

Know Your Guests
or
The Psychologist's Revenge

> **Most of the time you have people round that you know fairly well. However, you sometimes have to entertain completely new people – it may be someone's partner (partner: modern word meaning boyfriend/girlfriend/husband/wife/courtesan), a business associate or a neighbour.**

The traditional topics to avoid at the dinner table were Politics, Sex and Religion. These days sex can usually be discussed without too much danger but religion and politics are still a problem. If your guests know each other well and can be relied upon for a lively but non-violent discussion then don't worry. However, it is a good idea to avoid having people to dinner with wildly opposing views or beliefs if they are at all prone to talk about them. Blood does tend to spoil the napkins.

Similarly, recently divorced/divorcing couples can represent a serious hazard to the serenity of the occasion. If possible, invite the combatants to separate events, possibly get another friend to invite out the 'other' partner to reduce the risk of embarrassing clashes.

Regular guests are easier; you get to know what they like/don't like and it's really just making sure that you don't serve them the same meal every time. You are on safe ground here – you can even risk the odd experiment with the food. Another aspect to regular guests is that you will know if they tend to turn up on time/early/late and will be able to make allowances accordingly when cooking. You will have a good idea as to how late they like to stay and be able to pace the meal to suit.

Vegetarians/Vegans It is a genuine disaster if you don't find out about this beforehand. Vegans are even more tricky. It is one of life's sad truths that vegetarians expect you to have rustled up something fantastic for them in the line of buckwheat casserole, but that they never serve you a nicely cooked Steak au Poivre. But life is like that – there is no one as selfish as a religious/political/ethical convert. You just have to make allowances; they won't. So find out first. Vegetable curries are a good bet for these circumstances.

Allergies and special diets These are more commonplace than a lot of people think (even more common in the USA for some reason). Some are fashionable, others are real. We are both allergic to shellfish, and even people we know well forget from time to time and it is just as embarrassing for the guests as it is for the host to discover that one course is inedible. Some allergies, like fish/shellfish, potato, almonds and dairy products are fairly easy to get round as long as you know about them to start with. Medical problems such as kidney disease (which requires low/no salt) and diabetics (sugar has to be restricted) are more difficult. Get them to tell you what to cook and if necessary prepare a meal specially for them. When you do serve a different meal to one of your guests, do it discreetly and without fuss.

Food freaks and demon dieters People who, for no medical or religious/ethical reason, are fashionably faddy about what they will/won't eat are a problem. We just don't bother feeding them and see them elsewhere for drinks and so forth. Fortunately we don't know many folk in this category. Our advice is not to try and feed such folk, more importantly, don't let them cook for you; it will probably be awful. Tofu is only suitable for making wallpaper paste in our opinion.

Children and babies People's attitudes to offspring vary. Most will let you know if they need to bring theirs with them. The age and number will give you an idea what you have to do. Electric fences cope with most small babies. Older children, five is a dangerous age Cynthia, require more effective precautions. Once they get to about fifteen they can usually be expected to join in the proceedings, and you can even upset their parents by getting them drunk if you feel like it.

Smoking

There are people with a violent objection to smoking. If you know any of these then make sure that you don't have any smokers present at the same meal. If you smoke yourself then you won't invite them anyway. Make sure that there is an ashtray for each smoker – it saves getting the stuff on the carpet.

Drinking

There is always the business of drinking and driving (you shouldn't). If any of your guests have to drive make sure you have a supply of non-intoxicating fluid to keep them busy if not happy. There are people who choose not to drink by choice. (*Vita sine vinum morsa est* is what we say, or at least we might if we were Ancient Romans.) Again you need to make provision for these folk; giving them a bottle of designer water isn't really enough. Excess can also be a problem. It might be sensible to 'run out of' the hard stuff if you have someone who tends to go several over the eight and so restrict him/her to wine. They can always go home and get pixilated if they really need to, and it won't spoil anyone else's evening.

People who don't speak English

This is fortunately rare. Everyone has given up on the British and decided to learn English, with the exception of the Americans. But from time to time it does happen, and this is difficult. If some of the guests don't speak the language, the party tends to fragment into foreign and English speakers, not the best way of spending an evening. Choose the guests accordingly if you can. If you don't speak their language then you're in real trouble – go and hide.

Finally, the psychology of eating. The world is divided into two groups of people; those who believe the world can be split into groups and those who don't. Psychologists come into the former category, in particular they like to take ordinary words like 'theorist' and weigh them down with deep and hidden significance.

(I refuse to have anything to do with these scurrilous attacks on a noble profession; you should be silver-tongued and use honeyed words of praise. – S.)

(That's because you are a psychologist. – D.)

Anyway here is the psychologist's guide to eating styles:

Activist eaters These people like to taste a little of all the foods on their plate straight away. They are the first to show enthusiasm for, or criticism of, the meal. Unfortunately they are easily distracted and soon lose interest in the task at hand; they are poor finishers. You can recognise them by the amount of food left on the plate at the end of each course and their delight at the serving of the next course. These seemingly contradictory actions are perfectly normal for activists. Do not be put off. The ideal meals for these people are fondues, barbecues and buffets where they can nibble at lots of new things and so avoid boredom.

Pragmatist eaters It doesn't much matter what you give these people – they see eating as a means to an end and will proceed through each course in an impressive and practical manner. Whatever you put in front of them will be eaten, and they will not show any great gastronomic appreciation. They will comment on the sustaining qualities and its suitability for the time of year/weather conditions and so forth. They are not rewarding to cook for, but on the other hand they are not troublesome either. Feed them lots of good plain food, such as roast lamb and steamed puddings.

Theorist eaters They like to know all the details and will take time to find out everything they can about the food and drink on offer. They are easily recognisable as they will always ask for recipes and methods. If they are inclined to wine (Whine not?) they will want to know not only the vintage but the shipper and the types of grapes involved. They eat at a slower pace than activists or pragmatists and will seldom be the first to finish, though they will usually complete each course. Feed them quality food, accurately cooked, and be prepared to answer questions during the meal. It is always interesting to feed these people.

Reflective eaters Possibly the best people to cook for, they take their time savouring the flavours and balances of the meal. They are slow eaters and can be differentiated from theorists by the things they say. Reflecters will talk more about what they feel about the food; they will tend to romantic comparisons such as, 'like an angel's wings caressing your tongue'. You will get the maximum reward from these people when you present them with the ultimate gastronomic experience. Feed them food which is a treat to the eye as well as the stomach. They respond well to candlelight and gentle background music.

Here's the **Know Your Guests** checklist

Are they vegetarian/vegan?
Are they allergic to anything (children, for example)?
Do they have any special dietary requirements, e.g. diabetic?
What did you feed them last time?
Do they need soft drinks instead of/as well as booze?
Will they be bringing small children/babies?
Do they tend to be late/early/on time?
Do they tend to leave early/late?
Are they prone to getting drunk?
Are they burdened with strong political/religious views?
Does anyone have a violent objection to smoking?
Are any guests mutually exclusive (e.g. divorced couple)?

Acknowledgements
Who What and Why

Many people have participated, reviewed, edited, cajoled, encouraged, harassed and generally helped us in writing this book. This is where they get their bit of immortality on the printed page; they deserve it.

Clare Bristow of NEL for publishing us.
Jennifer and Lutz Luithlen for all sorts of things.
Sarah Judge for a magnificent pudding and grammar.
Steve Breibart for doing as he was told in the kitchen.
David's mother for recipes and providing David.
Buckinghams the Butchers for advice and meat.
Roger and Kim Wade Walker for illustrations and advice.
Glenn Duppenthaler for being the perfect hostess.
James Duppenthaler, 'Geneva Wine Expert'.
Davina for lettuce-throwing.
The writers of all the cookery books we have read over the years; some of their ideas are surely in here somewhere.

David's Elonex (TM) computer and Suzy's IBM (TM) computer which worked harder than anyone. We couldn't have done it without you, particularly when you let us play silly games during the boring bits.

Appendix A

Weights and Measures
or
How Many Mickles Mak a Muckle?

We've given all our measurements in metric and imperial units. For those who wish to convert to cups/American measures, or just want to check our arithmetic, here are some conversion tables (the cups are based on our own).

Table 1   Grammes and Ounces (1 gm = 0.035 oz, 1 oz = 28.35 gm)

For convenience when weighing, approximations have been made

Ounces		Grammes
1		25
2		50
3		75
4		110
5		150
6		175
7		200
8		225
9		250
10		275
11		300
12		350
13		375
14		400
15		425
16 =	1 lb	450
	2 lb	900
	4 lb	1800
	5 lb	2250
	10 lb	4500

(1 kg = 2¼ lb; 5 kg = 11 lb)

Table 2 Fluid Ounces/Pints Millilitres/Litres
(1 fl oz = 28.5 ml, 1 ml = .035 fl oz)
(1 pint = 0.57 litres, 1 litre = 1.76 pints)

Millilitres	to Fl Oz	Fl Oz	to Millilitres (ml)
10	½	1	25
25	1	2	50
50	2	3	75
75	3	4	110
100	4	5	150
200	7	6	175
300	10	7	200
400	15	8	230
500	20	9	270
750	30	10	300
1000 = 1 litre	35	15	400
		20 = 1 pint	600

Table 3 Oven Temperatures

Centigrade/Celsius	Fahrenheit	Regulo (gas mark)
70	150	
80	175	
100	200	low
110	225	¼
130	250	½
140	275	1
150	300	2
170	325	3
180	350	4
190	375	5
200	400	6
220	425	7
230	450	8
240	475	9
250	500	

Alternative measures:

The standard tall beer can holds 440 ml of beer. Empty (and thoroughly rinsed out) it holds the same volume of any other liquid. Small cans hold 275 ml.

Full jam jars make good additional weights for the scales when you need to weigh heavier objects.

The standard cup holds . . .

Unfortunately, there is nothing as non-standard as a cup, but people do like to use them as measures. If you want to calibrate your cups, then here is a 'home scientist' way to do it. You will need a large casserole, a pint measure (a milk bottle or container) and the cup of your choice. First, count how many pints of water you can get into the saucepan by repeatedly emptying the pint measure into it. Don't worry if there's a bit over or under, we're only after an accuracy of about 10 to 20 per cent. Empty the pan and repeat the operation using the cup. Count how many cups full are required to fill the casserole. Divide the number of pints by the number of cups to find out what fraction of a pint the cup holds. If this process doesn't put you off messing about with silly measures, then nothing will, so buy a measuring jug anyway.

Hint: For those of you who like a touch of the bizarre with your cooking, then a 34 B bra cup holds about 4 oz/100 gm of rice or granulated sugar – flour tends to fall through the holes. Likewise water.

Appendix B

Safety First in the Kitchen
or
Is there a Doctor in the House?

More accidents happen in the kitchen than any other room in the house. It's not surprising when you think of all the hazards that live there. Boiling water, sharp knives, hot fat for frying, gas jets, red hot rings, slippery floors, electrical appliances . . . it's amazing any of us survive and that's without considering food poisoning. The nearest we've come to disaster is setting fire to a stockpot (we forgot about it) and a badly cut finger on a new kitchen knife. These are our ideas on safety, both prevention and cure. Remember that prevention is better than cure.

Note: The First Aid information is only intended for help with very minor injuries; you should always get expert help for anything other than trivial incidents. When in doubt, get help.

Hint: Some people may try to get out of cooking by suggesting that it's much too dangerous in the kitchen. Just give them this appendix to read and tell them to be brave and get back in there.

Prevention:

MAINTENANCE — Make sure that all electrical appliances have a properly wired plug with the correct fuse in it. Check cables for fraying and keep clean and free of grease. Toasters and grills should be regularly emptied of crumbs and so forth.
The more complex appliances, such as freezers, refrigerators and ovens should be regularly inspected and serviced. The refrigerator is the most neglected machine in the kitchen. It sits there making the occasional whirring noise and everyone assumes that it's working just fine. In fact, it does need adjustment to cope with different weather conditions and can lose efficiency with old age. The answer is to invest in a thermometer — any one that goes down to 0°C/32°F will

be adequate. Then you can glance at it once in a while and make sure things are cold enough – it should be about 2° to 3°C/35° to 37°F. A couple of degrees above this and the rate of bacterial growth increases significantly. Occasionally, empty the refrigerator and wipe down with a suitable disinfecting cleaner. If you are ever in doubt about something in the refrigerator then throw it away, don't eat it.

Similar advice applies to deep freezes, except they should be much colder!

GENERAL HYGIENE

Keep everything as clean as possible. Worktops should be regularly wiped down with a mild disinfectant. Keep the floor clean and don't let crumbs lurk in corners; it only tempts the mice and cat food is a much better way of keeping the mogs happy. You should make sure that your hands are properly clean when preparing or serving food.

COOKED AND UNCOOKED FOOD

Particularly fish, flesh and fowl must be kept separate, otherwise the creepy crawlies from the raw stuff will make a rapid leap to the cooked food and you run a serious risk of poisoning. Do not handle cooked food after uncooked without washing your hands.

PETS

These love kitchens. Our cats spend the vast majority of their waking hours there, particularly when we're in there. Wonder why? However, they do represent a health and a physical hazard. You must make sure that they never go on worktops. Yes we know this is difficult with monkeys but be firm. Also make sure you know where they are before you start moving any hot liquids/fat about so that you don't trip and risk injury to you, as well as to them. Always check cookers, freezers and so on for the presence of wayward critters before operating them. Vets' bills are enormouse (Ho-Ho). And you can't thaw pets out by putting them in the oven either.

BOILING LIQUIDS AND HOT OIL | Scalds are very nasty things. Spill a pan of boiling oil on yourself and you'll quickly realise why it was so popular for dealing with medieval tax collectors. Never move boiling water/oil unless you absolutely have to. Make sure that it is in a stable place and make sure that anyone else in the kitchen knows where it is. Always use an oven glove or similar cloth to pick up the pan. Make sure you know where you are going to put it before you pick it up, and that the place is suitable (i.e. don't balance it on the edge of a table).

SAFETY EQUIPMENT | The kitchen is a good place to keep the first-aid box, then it is ready to hand when disaster strikes. You should also keep a fire extinguisher, CO_2 (Carbon Dioxide) ones are suitable. If you do, then make sure everyone who uses the kitchen knows how it works and make sure that it is checked regularly. A fire blanket (for keeping the fire warm?) comes in handy for smothering burning pans.

Cure for those things you couldn't quite prevent

Note: The information given here is intended to help you deal with small problems and prevent them becoming major ones. However, if the problem has become major, or you are not feeling confident, call for professional help.

BURNS (DRY) | These get caused by a variety of things – gas flames, hot surfaces such as saucepans/ovens/electric elements. They are of two types – superficial and deep. Superficial burns are ones in which only the outer layer of the skin is damaged; these hurt the most but are the least serious. Deep burns are where the inner and outer layers of the skin have been damaged. This includes the pain sensors, so these do not hurt as much. However, they are more serious. Always get expert help if you suspect a deep burn.

What to do. First remove the cause of the burn. If it was a hot pan you will probably have done this yourself by dropping it. Second, soak the burnt part with cold water, preferably flowing from a tap, and leave it there for at least ten minutes, preferably longer. This takes the heat out of the burn and reduces further damage. This is very important and makes a substantial difference to the subsequent injury. You should then remove any rings or other constricting articles from the area of the burn. If you don't do this then subsequent swelling may restrict blood flow – a bad thing. Last of all, apply a dry dressing to prevent infection. Where the burns are serious then the patient should be given small cold drinks to reduce the effect of shock.

If the burn is at all serious you must get help. If it is very serious, then an ambulance should be called. You must be careful not to pull away burnt skin, not to burst blisters or apply ointment.

Scalds

These are caused by moist heat such as boiling water, hot fat or steam. These are the most likely cause of serious injury from heat in the kitchen.

What to do. Essentially this is the same as for burns. However, with scalds it is likely that clothing has become soaked in boiling liquid. This should be carefully removed as quickly as possible. The affected part should be placed under cold running water or soaked in cold water for at least ten minutes. Rings and so forth should be removed from the affected area and a dry dressing applied. Serious scalds require hospital treatment as quickly as possible. Get an ambulance.

Burns (chemical)

In the kitchen these will usually be caused by a corrosive substance used in cleaning (many oven cleaners use caustic soda). The emphasis in treating these injuries is on speed. The affected area should be flooded with water to wash away the chemical. Any clothing which has become soaked with chemical should be removed. Then treat as for a burn.

CUTS AND GRAZES   These are about the most common injuries in the kitchen. Sharp knives, graters and machines with whirling blades can all do damage if concentration is lost. Minor cuts, where there is only a little bleeding, and light grazes can be treated very simply by rinsing with cold water, drying the skin with cotton wool or clean kitchen towel (applied gently), and then using a simple plaster or dressing. More serious cuts, where the bleeding is profuse and doesn't show much sign of stopping, need more complex treatment, get help.

ELECTRIC SHOCK   The last of the medical emergencies we cover; the squeamish can open their eyes and start reading again. (There was something a little illogical about that sentence.) Do not touch the patient until the source of the electricity has been removed, i.e. turn off the switch/pull out the plug/turn off the mains supply at the fuse box. Take great care in doing this as it doesn't help anyone if you get an electric shock too. Then treat any burns as described. If the patient is unconscious or in need of artificial respiration then, unless you know what you are doing, get expert help.

FIRE   Three things are required to start a fire: fuel, oxygen and a source of ignition. Once it's got going it only needs fuel and oxygen, and that's how you stop it – by depriving it of one or both. In the kitchen the most likely things to catch fire are frying pans, saucepans and clothing. As long as you act quickly and calmly, then all of these can be easily dealt with. However, once any of these gets out of hand it is amazing just how flammable a kitchen is – worktops, gas, floor coverings, wooden cupboards are all first rate fuels. So nip the problem in the bud. If you have a fire extinguisher in the kitchen (*see* **Prevention**) use it.

Note: Ordinary smoke detectors are unsuitable for the kitchen. If you want one, get a special one designed for use in a kitchen.

Frying pan and saucepan fires
: First of all turn off the source of heat. Do not try to pick it up. Do not pour water on it. Do smother the flames with a fire blanket or a suitably large saucepan lid (some frying pans have their own lid – use this). Leave it to cool down until it is cold enough to take to the sink for, if possible, restoration to a usable state.

Clothing
: If part of your clothing goes on fire, then get away from the cause (gas ring, most likely one) and remove the clothing as quickly as possible. If you are on your own rolling on the floor to smother the flames is the best policy. Treat any burns as described under that heading.

If a fire has got out of hand then don't try and deal with it yourself; evacuate the kitchen, closing the door behind you, leave the premises, taking everyone with you and call the fire brigade.

Burnt (boiled dry) saucepans
: Provided they are thick-bottomed, and they haven't been holed, they are usually retrievable. Spray-on oven cleaners (read the directions) can often be used effectively for cleaning off burnt offerings; wear rubber gloves for protection. Caustic soda (again read the directions and dispose of carefully and wear rubber gloves for protection as it is extremely corrosive), wire wool or an abrasive pad can be used for removing the stubborn bits.